The Gig Public

The Gig Public

AI-Driven Contractual and Habitual Performativisation of Publicness

Slavko Splichal

ANTHEM PRESS

ANTHEM PRESS

Anthem Press
An imprint of Wimbledon Publishing Company
www.anthempress.com

This edition first published in UK and USA 2026
by ANTHEM PRESS
75–76 Blackfriars Road, London SE1 8HA, UK
or PO Box 9779, London SW19 7ZG, UK
and
244 Madison Ave #116, New York, NY 10016, USA

British Library Cataloguing-in-Publication Data
A catalogue record for this book is available from the British Library.

Library of Congress Cataloging-in-Publication Data: 2025940366
A catalog record for this book has been requested.

ISBN-13: 978-1-83999-521-7 (Hbk)/ 978-1-83999-522-4 (Pbk)
ISBN-10: 1-83999-521-1 (Hbk)/ 1-83999-522-X (Pbk)

Cover Credit: Image courtesy of Peter Maček, Ljubljana

This title is also available as an eBook.

CONTENTS

FOREWORD

A few months after the publication of my book *Datafication of the Public Sphere and Public Opinion* in 2022, the world was irrevocably altered by the arrival of OpenAI's ChatGPT. Its debut in November 2022 sent shockwaves across industries and academia alike, igniting an intense global conversation about its vast potential and profound implications. Everywhere, people speculated about the transformative possibilities of generative AI – from its promise to revolutionise education and creativity to its potential risks for employment, misinformation and even the nature of human cognition. AI, at once exhilarating and formidable, now stands poised to reshape how we work, learn, conduct business, access healthcare and – perhaps most radically – how we communicate with one another.

Nowhere was this reckoning felt more acutely than in the world of news and media. Journalists, editors and media executives recognised that AI was not just another technological wave but a transformative force capable of redrawing the very contours of their profession. Across the globe, news organisations rushed to develop AI strategies or expand existing ones, caught between the dazzling promise of AI-driven innovation and the daunting challenge of preserving media integrity, public discourse and democratic engagement.

Just weeks before ChatGPT's release, I had completed a paper on 'contractual publics'. Yet, as the implications of generative AI began to unfold, I felt compelled to rethink and revisit my work. This rethinking ultimately gave rise to the present book, which explores the emergence of what I call the 'gig public'. Initially, I welcomed AI as a creative partner and a wellspring of knowledge. But as I delved deeper into how these technologies shape public discourse, my initial optimism was tempered by growing concerns – especially about the risks of epistemic fragmentation and the exacerbation of social polarisation. This tension between democratic possibility and disruptive peril has profoundly shaped the thinking behind this book.

As I immersed myself in this project, I continually grappled with the rapid evolution and far-reaching impact of digital technologies and AI tools on the fundamental, historically grounded attributes of public opinion. Tools like

ChatGPT are not just changing how we communicate – they are also reshaping the frameworks through which we, as scholars and citizens, engage with our own research and our shared reality. In this sense, the book reflects an intellectual journey that unfolds alongside a technological revolution – one that challenges core concepts such as publicness, communication, opinion formation and even democracy itself. The tectonic shifts triggered by AI are disrupting long-standing epistemic structures forged in the pre-digital era, challenging the habitual practices, contractual interactions and public reasoning, which I see as core constituents of the formation of the public and public opinion in both pre-digital and contemporary communified societies.

Throughout this journey, I have remained both cautious and hopeful. I am energised by AI's potential to help us rethink traditional models of publicness and democratic participation. Yet I am equally convinced that this potential can only be realised through vigilance, ethical commitment and a clear resolve to ensure that these technologies serve the many rather than the privileged few. If there is one conviction that has crystallised for me, it is this: for all its power, AI remains a reflection of the people and institutions that create and wield it. The responsibility to guide its development with care and conscience rests with us – as scholars, citizens and co-creators of our digital future.

The challenges we face are immense, and their solutions far from straightforward. I do not pretend to have resolved them in these pages. But I hope this book offers both a critical inquiry and a call to action – an invitation to engage ethically, creatively and courageously with the forces that will shape our shared futures.

This work is not mine alone. It stands on a foundation of collaboration and dialogue. I am deeply grateful to my academic friends, critical colleagues, reviewers and proofreaders, whose insights and generosity have shaped this work at every stage. In particular, I wish to thank Murray Bales, Bart Cammaerts, Bob Ivie, Risto Kunelius, Hannu Nieminen and Philip Schlesinger, as well as to my colleagues at the Centre for Social Communication Research of the Faculty of Social Sciences, the University of Ljubljana.

I also wish to acknowledge the many scholars, thinkers and practitioners whose ideas have shaped and enriched my own. The ongoing conversation about publicness, AI and democracy is evolving rapidly, and I am humbled to contribute to it. For many years, I have had the privilege of working alongside the editorial board of *Javnost – The Public*, a journal I have been honoured to edit for more than thirty years. Their commitment to critical thought and intellectual rigor continues to inspire me.

Furthermore, I would like to extend my appreciation to the AI tools that assisted me in the development of this book. Their support in brainstorming ideas, refining concepts and offering feedback has been invaluable. While this book is ultimately my own, the assistance and tools provided by this technology have played an important role in helping me shape and clarify my thoughts.

My gratitude also extends to the Slovenian Research and Innovation Agency for the financial support that made this work possible.

Finally, I am deeply grateful to the living beings in my Ljubljana home for their vibrant life energy and heartfelt kindness, which I have been fortunate to receive for so long. Their presence has been a constant source of encouragement and joy. Above all, I extend my love and gratitude to my life companion, Zorica, for her patience, unwavering support and care – throughout this project and throughout our life together.

Ljubljana, March 2025

INTRODUCTION

The Gig Public – Rethinking
Publicness in the Age of AI

The rapid advancements in artificial intelligence (AI) in recent years have fundamentally reshaped our perception of technological progress, heralding a new era of innovation unlike anything seen before. AI's unique ability to perform complex tasks that were once considered exclusively human – such as reasoning, decision-making and problem-solving – has brought about profound and long-term societal consequences, surpassing the transformative effects of previous technological milestones, such as the microprocessor, personal computer, Internet and mobile phone.

Unlike previous technological revolutions, which primarily enhanced human productivity and connectivity, AI goes a step further by introducing systems capable of autonomously learning, reasoning and adapting. This shift marks a departure from tools that merely extend human capabilities to systems that independently process vast amounts of data, make complex decisions and anticipate outcomes, often exceeding human capacity in various domains. AI systems are designed to continually improve their performance over time without human intervention, fundamentally changing how humans live, work, consume, spend their leisure time and interact with the world.

AI's impact goes well beyond the technological realm, signalling a deep societal transformation that is set to influence the very essence of human society. Its integration into key sectors like healthcare, education, transportation and communication is already revolutionising traditional systems, offering unparalleled opportunities for efficiency, innovation and an improved quality of life. Still, this transformative potential also brings considerable challenges with it, including the need to address critical issues such as ethical governance, algorithmic bias and ensuring equitable access.

Among the key phenomena transformed by AI, publicness occupies a critical position. The transformative impacts of AI on publicness, publicity, public opinion and the public sphere within democratic societies are undeniable. However, the nature and extent of these consequences can only be fully grasped when approached from a historical perspective.

Publicness has always been tied to the mechanisms via which individuals and groups interact, share ideas and shape decision-making processes. Over time, its evolution has been marked by transformative technological milestones: the invention of the printing press, the industrialisation of the press, the rise of broadcast media and the advent of the Internet. Each of these developments reshaped how information was circulated, how publics were constituted and how power was distributed within societies. Yet, AI introduces a qualitatively different transformation – one that goes beyond merely mediating and shaping public discourse to actively generating it and challenging its foundational principles.

A historical perspective helps contextualise this shift. Just as the industrialisation of the press brought both the democratisation and commodification of information, AI extends this duality. While on the one hand, it gives unprecedented opportunities for participation and personalised communication, on the other, it fosters fragmentation, epistemic enclaves and susceptibility to manipulation via opaque algorithmic processes. Understanding AI's role in influencing publicness today thus calls for examining how historical transitions have impacted the power dynamics, agency and vulnerabilities of publics.

In this new paradigm, publicness is transformed to become a hybrid construct moulded by human interaction and algorithmic intervention. This transformation disrupts traditional understandings of collective engagement and societal consensus, requiring a fundamental reassessment of publicness as a concept. Situated at the nexus of technology, power and social relations, publicness in the age of AI challenges the foundational principles of democratic dialogue and civic participation. By embedding the analysis of AI's impact on publicness within a historical context, a clearer picture can emerge concerning both the continuities and disruptions in how technology mediates the relationships between individuals, society and democratic institutions.

This monograph looks at the transformations in the multifaceted nature of the public and its dynamic relationships with other societal structures, focusing on the shifting boundaries between public and private domains in the age of digitisation and communification. Also explored is how critical theory has responded to these transformations, shedding light on how contemporary developments are redefining civic engagement and the essence of public life in an ever more interconnected yet fragmented world. Central to this analysis is a consideration of the interplay between habits, customs, the will to visibility, negotiations and contractual relationships that simultaneously complement and diverge from the normatively privileged domain of public reasoning. Such dynamics challenge conventional ideals of publicness, complicating traditional frameworks that principally view it through the lens of rational deliberation and collective consensus.

From these two perspectives – shifting the public/private boundary and the nature of public reasoning – the study is structured around three primary focal points. First, it analyses how new *information and communication technologies* alter human interactions within the public and private spheres. Second, it examines the influence of *capitalist economic dynamics* and governmentality strategies on reshaping the public realm, fundamentally altering the nature of the public and its democratic potential. Third, it looks at how *habitual and contractual practices* traditionally associated with the private sphere profoundly influence the ongoing evolution of publicness.

The monograph aims to provide a comprehensive analysis of the challenges stemming from the fragmentation of contemporary public discourse and the emergence of *gig publics* – digitally mediated, algorithmically structured discursive networks in which human–algorithm interactions unfold through short bursts of attention and performative expression. Shaped more by habitual behaviour and platform-driven incentives than sustained dialogue or collective deliberation, gig publics blur the boundary between public and private life, complicating traditional notions of publicness. By exploring the fluid and often unstable character of gig publics, which proliferate within underdeveloped forms of crypto-, proto- or pseudo-public spheres (Splichal 2012, 161), the book also seeks to identify effective strategies for invigorating or reinventing publicness and fostering more meaningful public engagement.

With the recent digital expansion of the public's social base, driven by increased Internet accessibility and social media proliferation, one might expect the public's critical role to broaden, amplifying a diversity of voices and strengthening democratic participation. Yet, paradoxically, the opposite effect seems to prevail. Instead of cultivating a more robust, engaged public, we are witnessing its gradual decline.

This trend is starkly illustrated by the contrasting paths of two key figures in the digital transformation of publicness – Julian Assange and Mark Zuckerberg. Both considerably influenced how we perceive and engage with the public sphere at the turn of the millennium, yet their visions and legacies could not be further apart. These two paths illuminate a larger paradox in digital publicness, where the potential for empowerment and democratic engagement is increasingly marginalised by the competing forces of commodification, performativisation and the surveillance of public life.

In the 2010 *Time* magazine's Person of the Year poll, WikiLeaks founder Julian Assange emerged as the clear favourite, receiving the most votes and outpacing Facebook founder Mark Zuckerberg, who ranked only tenth. Nevertheless, it was Zuckerberg who was ultimately named *Time*'s

2010 Person of the Year, recognised 'for affecting the lives of more than half a billion people'. Still, this outcome sparked debate and criticism regarding *Time* magazine's choice, as wittily captured by comedian Bill Hader during his final Saturday Night Live show of 2010. In a satirical portrayal of Assange and his surprise at the award being given to Zuckerberg, Hader humorously noted the irony: 'What are the differences between Mark Zuckerberg and me [Assange]? I give you private information on corporations for free and I'm a villain. Zuckerberg gives your private information to corporations for money and he's Man of the Year.'

This staged dialogue reveals the profound implications of the divergent paths taken by Assange and Zuckerberg. WikiLeaks, through its bold revelations of governmental and corporate misconduct, has held the potential to instigate lasting and transformative effects on publicness and democracy – far surpassing Facebook's achievement of 'affecting the lives of more than half a billion people'. By exposing the inner workings of power and shedding light on the hidden truths that are worthy of public scrutiny – made possible through an open Internet platform – WikiLeaks challenged the status quo by demanding greater transparency and accountability from those in power and inviting traditional (news) media to fulfil their role as 'organs of the public'. In so doing, it has prompted a global reckoning with the ethical and political dimensions of secrecy, surveillance and the right to information, leaving a profound impact on how we (can) perceive social media, politics and diplomatic relations between governments. Assange's work, while deemed controversial by his critics, aligns with the Enlightenment normative ideals of using publicness to empower citizens, to raise awareness of the importance of transparency and the integrity of rulers in their interactions with citizens and to prevent excesses of power.

In contrast, Zuckerberg's Facebook, while undeniably influential on a global scale, has been critiqued for fostering a more superficial form of public engagement. Facebook's business model, which bypasses traditional media to secretly extract, manipulate and monetise user data while facilitating targeted advertising, has been widely criticised for its role in the commodification of personal information. This model has contributed to a major shift in the nature of privacy and its reconceptualisation, favouring corporate privacy – shielding business interests and proprietary algorithms – at the expense of genuine personal privacy. The platform's role in prioritising profit through the exploitation of user data, spreading misinformation, creating echo chambers and amplifying divisive content has heightened concerns about surveillance, consent and the broader implications for the quality of public discourse and the health of democracy. Yet, irrespective of these criticisms, Zuckerberg has ascended to become one of the world's wealthiest individuals by capitalising

on the sale of personal data. Meanwhile, Assange languished in imprison-
ment in the United Kingdom, faced with the threat of spending life in prison
for his endeavours to make governments more transparent if extradited to
the United States. He was eventually released after a plea deal with the US
government in June 2024.

Hader's staged dialogue offers a compelling illustration of the consequences arising from the stark contrast between the Enlightenment's normative conceptualisations of publicness and the public embodied by Assange's
advocacy for transparency and the emerging forms of publicness shaped by
social media platforms, exemplified by Zuckerberg's business model. At the
core of this contrast lies the paradox Hader highlighted – while Zuckerberg is
heralded as virtuous, Assange is vilified.

The cases of WikiLeaks and Facebook are only the tip of the iceberg when
it comes to changes in publicness over recent decades. The contrast between
Assange and Zuckerberg shows a broader shift in how publicness and public-
worthiness – oscillating between information-as-power (e.g., WikiLeaks) and
information-as-commodity (e.g., Facebook) – are perceived and assessed in
the digital age within Western democracies. Why is exposing the abuse of
power deemed to be a threat to democratic governance, both politically and
legally, whereas (re)producing trivial chatter is, at best, viewed as fostering
social engagement and enhancing access to the public sphere or, at worst,
dismissed as inconsequential given its lack of immediate political impact?
In a country often hailed as the cradle of modern democracy, which factors have contributed to such divergent evaluations of these two innovations
and interventions in the public sphere? How did this great social turn in the
perception and assessment of public-worthiness emerge, diverging so sharply
from Enlightenment ideals?

The answers to these questions lie in understanding the complex interplay of the evolving nature of communication technologies, the economic
interests that drive them and the shifting cultural norms that impact our
understanding of public discourse. It is also important to recognise that the
Enlightenment's normative principle of publicness was never fully realised
in practice. Modern transformations of publicness represent a radical departure from Enlightenment ideals, which stressed the crucial role of publicity
in safeguarding human freedoms and democracy. Enlightenment thinkers
placed their trust in human reason and believed in the power of public discourse as a means of challenging authority, promoting transparency and
holding rulers accountable. They valued the public exchange of opinions
and arguments, viewing it as essential for the functioning of a democratic
society in which citizens could collectively deliberate on matters of common
interest. From their perspective, publicness and publicity were inherently

tied to rational thought and the protection of individual liberties within a democratic polity.

Digitalisation and Communification

Yet in modern conditions, the theory of the reasoned public – rooted in the values of Western civilisation, the Enlightenment and the ideal of universalism – encounters considerable difficulties. While the normative theory of the public, influenced by Enlightenment ideals, assumes a rational, dispassionate public with individuals discussing and deliberating on matters of common concern, it fails to account for the emotional and affective dimensions of political life, as well as the inherent conflicts arising from diverse interests and competing wills to power. In consequence, the model of publicness that champions reason and universalism above all else proves inadequate for capturing the complexities of contemporary public engagement, regenerating the public from deep crisis and rehabilitating its epistemic value.

In this developing context, social media platforms have emerged as multifaceted spaces that are integral to daily life, serving as hubs for a wide range of activities that span both private and public spheres. Originally designed as venues for personal connection and entertainment, these platforms now play a significant role across many dimensions of modern life, blurring the boundaries between business, leisure, civic engagement and political discourse. For businesses, social media is a key tool for marketing, customer engagement, brand building and e-commerce, allowing companies to reach global audiences with unmatched ease and precision. Simultaneously, these platforms offer individuals a space for leisure, permitting them to share personal experiences, connect with friends and family and consume content adjusted to their interests.

However, the utility of social media extends far beyond business and leisure activities. It has become a vital space for civic engagement and political initiatives where citizens can organise, mobilise and advocate for social and political causes. From grassroots movements to global campaigns, social media facilitates the rapid dissemination of information, the coordination of collective actions and the amplification of voices that might otherwise go unheard. Political discussions on social media have the power to shape public opinion, influence policy decisions and even alter the course of elections. While the changes driven by the platform economy hold the potential to foster new forms of engagement, democratise creative expression and empower a class of creative users or 'produsers' to make a living from their passions and enthusiasm embodied in the products, knowledge or content they sell – a quixotic idea that echoes early claims about the Internet's democratic potential – these platforms still generally treat users as customers rather than citizens.

The multifaceted nature of social media – as platforms and services that enable individuals to create, share and interact with content and engage in social networking – raises complex questions about their impact on democratic processes, the right to privacy and the nature of public discourse. Once celebrated as agents of freedom, social media have now become virtual public hubs of the twenty-first century where the boundaries between personal, professional and public are increasingly blurred, creating both opportunities and threats for individuals and society alike.

Critical attitudes towards Enlightenment normativism were already articulated in the late nineteenth and early twentieth centuries in the USA and Europe through critical sociology, which examined social structures and power dynamics relevant to the public and public opinion. Gabriel Tarde, Ferdinand Tönnies, John Dewey and several members of the Chicago School contributed significant insights into the importance of social interactions in influencing individuals and communities, laying the groundwork for understanding the complex interplay of individual, social and environmental factors in the development of public opinion.

In his normative or 'pure theoretical' system of elementary and complex forms of social will, Tönnies conceptualised the public and public opinion as detached from the legislative processes (the state) and contractual relations (the economy) that govern society yet also emphasised that different manifestations of social will are inherently 'mutually related and pass into each other' in real life, as studied through applied and empirical sociology. In contrast to economic interactions in *Gesellschaft* that are guided by *convention* and political life regulated by *legislation*, public opinion mostly pertains to the ethical – and, by extension, aesthetic – dimensions of common life, albeit it remains interconnected with both convention and legislation.

Like other critical sociologists of the time, Tönnies observed that public opinion – as an empirical process of the formation of social will – often reveals stark disparities in life circumstances, social positions and class divisions among participants. Public debates, far from being the egalitarian exchanges envisioned by Enlightenment thinkers, grant some individuals more freedom than others. These disparities – shaped by emotional attachments, shared grievances and collective experiences of injustice – result in unequal access to the resources needed for meaningful participation in public life, including political engagement and civic activities. This inequality is further exacerbated in the modern age of rapid technological development. Following Tönnies' argument, individuals with higher socio-economic status are more likely to have access to education, information and influential social networks, enabling them to exert greater influence in public debates. In contrast, those from marginalised backgrounds, particularly those with lower incomes, often struggle to have their voices heard, let alone taken seriously, in public debates.

Sociologists have extensively studied and empirically demonstrated the problems of inequality in the public sphere. Tom Harrisson (1940, 375), for example, highlighted a key contradiction in his distinction between 'private opinion' – understood as the immediate, often temporary opinions expressed by individuals to strangers – and 'published opinion', which refers to how these opinions are presented or represented in the media and Parliament. He argued that published opinion is frequently shaped by elite perspectives – typically formed and discussed in exclusive *clubs* – and does not reflect the genuine sentiments of the general populace. In contrast, these sentiments are more commonly articulated in the informal contexts of *pubs*. He concluded that 'there is no getting away from this fact: the Press and Parliament version of public opinion is frequently miles away from "real public opinion", let alone private opinion'.

Such unequal access for individuals to different sites of deliberation in the public sphere, along with the limited representation of diverse opinions in the media, raises important questions about the very legitimacy of public opinion and the authenticity and inclusiveness of democratic deliberation. When the public sphere is dominated by those with greater social and economic capital, existing power imbalances are reinforced, further marginalising the voices of those already marginalised. In turn, the public sphere risks becoming less a site for genuine democratic engagement and more a tool for fostering hierarchies and inequalities that already exist.

The complexities and contradictions of public opinion are growing in today's era of rapid *communification* – a phenomenon characterised by AI-curated digital interactions that seamlessly integrate online and offline virtual spaces. Communification refers to the profound integration of digital communication technologies into nearly all aspects of human life, where communication becomes not only more deeply embedded in most human activities than ever before but also extends beyond human-to-human interaction, facilitating communication between humans and machines.

In terms of importance and the scope of its transformative impact, communification can only be compared to the invention of writing. Writing, as one of the earliest epistemic and cognitive technologies, revolutionised the way knowledge was generated, preserved, transmitted and structured. As an *epistemic* technology – referring to shared knowledge systems – it externalised human memory, enabling knowledge to be stored, shared and critiqued across time and space. It laid the foundation for rational-critical deliberation and the expansion of collective knowledge. As a *cognitive* technology, writing transformed individual minds by allowing them to reduce memory burdens, acting as a 'mental prosthesis' for storing and recalling complex information. It facilitated abstract reasoning, planning and self-reflection, while shaping how individuals conceptualise the world through language. However, writing also introduced new complexities and contradictions. While it democratised access to knowledge for some, it also entrenched new forms of inequality, as literacy became a dividing line between those with access to information and those without. The technology of writing not only set the foundations for human civilisation but also for class-based societies.

The comparison between the consequences of writing and AI highlights a broader trajectory in the evolution of cognitive and epistemic technologies: from tools that merely extend human memory and rationality to systems that mediate communication and actively shape human thought and knowledge. Digital technologies, with AI as their most prominent example, represent a new frontier in epistemic technologies, building on and transcending the capabilities of earlier tools like writing. While writing externalised memory and facilitated critical reflection, AI augments cognitive capabilities by enabling dynamic information processing, pattern recognition and the generation of new content. This evolution creates opportunities for unprecedented creativity, efficiency and insight. However, it also amplifies contradictions, such as the erosion of shared epistemic foundations and the potential displacement of human expertise.

Communification has profoundly transformed how we communicate, conduct business, fulfil civic responsibilities and engage in political processes. These technologies have redefined the boundaries of the public and private spheres, with social media platforms, online shopping and data sharing increasingly blurring the lines that once clearly separated them. Beyond reshaping how public opinion is formed, they also redefine the very essence of publicness, raising urgent questions about inclusivity, representation and the balance between human agency and algorithmic influence.

This shift marks the end of what Norberto Bobbio (1980/1989) labelled 'the great public/private dichotomy' – a division he regarded as fundamental, akin to other dichotomies such as war and peace, democracy and autocracy, society and community and the state of nature and civil society. Still, it remains an open question whether these dichotomies ever truly existed or if they are merely polar values on a continuum of key dimensions in social relations. For example, Jeremy Bentham did not perceive the relationship between public and private as a straightforward dichotomy, but rather as a continuum, with privacy and publicness serving as crystalline values at either end. As he argued, neither publicness nor privateness constitutes a natural state or inherent property of entities. Instead, both are socially constructed and contingent, influenced by the specific contexts, purposes and societal norms in which they are enacted.

Regardless of how complexly publicness and privateness are conceptualised, communification has blurred their boundaries, causing them to intersect and making them more susceptible to corporate and political power than ever before. Just as complete privacy has always been utopian – and probably never socially desirable – so too is the idea of 'total publicness'. With the rise of big data, AI and human-machine interaction, privacy and publicness have become battlegrounds where efforts to redefine the 'demarcation lines' between them are shaped by the strategic interests of major political, economic and technological actors. The 'endpoint' of total privacy – where others have no knowledge of us, no attention directed at us, no physical access to us and no control over us – is as unattainable as the opposite (totalitarian) extreme on the multidimensional continuum: total publicness, which would entail global visibility, universal access, an all-binding discursive order, a singular public and a monolithic public opinion.

In any case, the continuity perspective seems more fitting in the context of Internet communications, where public and private are heavily intertwined and their boundaries often blurred. The content that is allowed to become public versus what must remain private in any given transaction now depends on determining what is deemed necessary for collective consideration and what, conversely, could disrupt the interaction if made publicly visible or accessible. Ultimately, the fundamental question is: Who holds the power to make these decisions?

Social media platforms, in particular, operate as complex ecosystems where formal, contractual agreements coexist with informal, habitual practices. This creates a dynamic environment that is in a constant state of flux, impacted by the mutual influence and adaptations of content creators, users and platforms. The pervasive influence of these digital arenas touches nearly every aspect of our lives, rendering them powerful instruments for positive change as well as potential sources of disruption, encapsulating the complexities and contradictions of our digital age.

While embracing these digital transformations, it is crucial to recognise the darker implications of modern instantiations of publicness, which are increasingly characterised by the erosion of human liberties and the unchecked concentration of power among the digital oligarchs of surveillance capitalism.[1] This shift is epitomised by the rise of tech giants who wield unparalleled

---

1 Surveillance capitalism is a term coined by Shoshana Zuboff (2019) to describe a new economic system centred on the unilateral extraction and analysis of personal data by corporations to predict, influence and monetise behaviour, often without meaningful consent.

influence over public discourse via their control of digital platforms. Rather than fostering reasoned debate and realms for meaningful democratic participation, these platforms often serve as tools for misinformation, manipulation, surveillance and coercion, deepening ideological divisions and eroding trust in democratic institutions. The once-cherished ideals of publicness, seen as vital for critical reflection and civic engagement, have been overshadowed by the controversial effects of 'gig communication' – a system driven by AI and algorithms that shifts and blurs the boundaries between public and private, prioritises profit over the public good and diminishes the role of autonomous human reasoning.

As society grapples with these technology-driven changes, it becomes increasingly important to revisit and critically engage with the Enlightenment principles that once guided conceptualisations of publicness. Yet, attributing the shifts in our understanding of publicness exclusively to recent technological revolutions would be overly simplistic. Normative ideas of the public have never had a consistent empirical counterpart throughout history. This observation applies not only to the foundational philosophical ideas about publicness established during the Enlightenment but also to the sociological theories developed in the late nineteenth and early twentieth centuries. Influential theorists and public intellectuals such as John Dewey and Ferdinand Tönnies underscored the historical assumptions embedded in theoretical conceptions of the public and public opinion, emphasising that without deliberate social efforts to bridge the gap between empirical realities and normative ideals, the concept of the public risks remaining a mere counterfactual ideal.

Historical configurations of the public often diverge significantly from normative ideals, as they frequently incorporate 'admixtures' of social relations that stand in opposition to the public. Critical sociologists at the turn of the nineteenth to the twentieth century noted that the *crowd* and, later, the *mass* not only represent empirical and conceptual antitheses to the public but also embody complex forms in which the potential for a public resides. Both the public and the mass hold the latent possibility of transforming into their opposite, underscoring the inherent dual nature – both an affirmation and a potential negation – of publicness. This duality suggests that our understanding of publicness must evolve with a keen awareness of this dynamic tension.

The Gig Public

In our quest to conceptualise a more realistic public, it is essential to critically analyse both the historical narratives and contemporary practices. This approach allows us to work towards a public that genuinely reflects democratic values, encouraging engagement and participation rather than succumbing to the forces of manipulation and control. The challenge lies not only in understanding the technological shifts but also in recognising the historical and social dimensions that have shaped the contours of publicness over time, along with the obstacles that have often hindered its genuine realisation.

Addressing the challenges of contemporary publicness calls for a rethinking of the theories of the public and the public sphere to account for the diverse and often conflicting interests, passions and identities that influence political life. It also demands a critical examination of how social and economic inequalities shape who participates in public discussions and whose voices are heard. By grappling with these complexities, we can move towards a more inclusive and democratic conception of the public sphere – one that not only reflects the diversity of contemporary society and embraces the plurality of experiences and perspectives within it but also critically identifies both the potential for and obstacles to the empowerment and cultivation of publics.

A critical consideration of the evolving nature of publicness in the digital worlds led me to conceptualise the 'gig public' as a new paradigm that challenges traditional understandings of the public and its role in shaping social and political change. Unlike conventional notions of publicness and the public, the gig public is characterised by habitual, spontaneous, transient, contractual and loosely structured engagement in public discourse – often hindered by the difficulties in fostering sustained interaction and in-depth discussion due to the fleeting, fragmented and performative nature of online interactions.

Why gig public? The concept alludes to the term *gig*, which is widely used in contemporary economic and popular discourse to describe temporary, fragmented, precarious and platform-mediated forms of work. As used in this book, gig public signals a shift away from stable, partially institutionalised forms of publicness towards fragmented, contractual and performative modes of public disclosure or exposure – of actions, events and symbolic processes – within mediated public spaces. The 'gig', as a metaphor, highlights episodic, datafied and platform-dependent forms of performative engagement. It also evokes a depoliticised temporariness: publics that coalesce and dissipate like a gig – a fleeting event rather than an enduring structure.[2]

Gig public is not a normative but an analytical concept, referring to the rapid formation of short-lived communicative relations in which multiple

---

2 The meaning of the word *gig* has evolved significantly since the eighteenth century, both as a noun and a verb. Its modern usage took shape in American slang in the 1920s, when a gig referred to a short-term performance by a musician or comedian. As a verb, *to gig* was (and sometimes still is) also used to mean 'to provoke'.

voices compete for attention within an oversaturated information environment. In this model, the public emerges as a fluid and performative phenomenon, drawing individuals together around shared interests, events or significant moments. These temporary 'assemblages' of engagement function less through sustained, reasoned debate and more through synchronised – often algorithmically co-generated – expressions of the will to visibility, emotion, affect or solidarity, resembling an audience responding in real-time to a concert. For example, by appending hashtags (#) to a term, users not only draw attention to a trending issue but also facilitate the automatic formation of a real-time collectivity composed of individuals who express interest by engaging with the tagged content.

The gig public reflects how digital technologies have reshaped the mechanisms of civic participation, muddying the boundaries between active engagement and passive consumption. Just as concertgoers may experience a powerful yet ephemeral sense of unity during a performance, a feeling that may persist for some time, participants in the gig public may also feel a fleeting connection or shared purpose. However, the lack of sustained interaction or organisational continuity often limits the potential for these moments to generate a significant social or political impact.

The gig public paradigm also highlights the challenges intrinsic to digital environments, including the prioritisation of spectacle and virality over substance, the dominance of platform algorithms in shaping collective attention and the difficulty of reconciling diverse perspectives within transient digital assemblies. By examining the gig public, we gain a deeper understanding of the interplay – and inherent contradictions – between performative immediacy, which encourages more active participant engagement, and the structural constraints on such engagement, which coalesce through algorithmic governance.

My introduction of the concept of gig publics marks a departure from conventional notions of the public and publicness by emphasising the roles of customs, negotiations, contracts and the will to visibility – elements that complement the normatively privileged public reasoning within public domains. Unlike the recent proliferation of descriptors – such as strong, weak, transnational, agonistic or online publics – that highlight specific aspects or evolutions of publics across diverse social and technological contexts, the term gig publics captures the generic characteristics of empirically emergent publics situated along Gabriel Tarde and Robert E. Park's 'mass–public continuum', which parallels Jeremy Bentham's 'private–public continuum'. The habitual and contractual attributes of publics, which have culminated in the surveillance economy, were already implicit in early conceptualisations of publics but have been largely neglected in later theories of the public sphere.

The concept of the gig public seeks to reclaim the critical epistemic value of publicness that has been eroded through the (conceptual) fragmentation of publics. It is not simply a metaphor for the episodic or atomised nature of public discourse under gig economy conditions. Nor is it a functionalist tool for maintaining social stability in complex societies – as in Pitirim Sorokin's notion of 'pseudo-public opinions of factions, sects and individuals' – or a descriptive label for propaganda and polling technologies used in opinion and attitude research, akin to Talcott Parsons' idea of 'automatic control mechanisms' designed to minimise disorganisation in complex social systems.

Rather, the gig public transcends these interpretations, offering a framework that critically examines how the structures of modern publicness are being reshaped in the age of AI. It draws from a rich sociological tradition of exploring the contradictory character of the public influenced by the habitual and contractual behaviour among its members. The concept of the gig public suggests an interaction between three seemingly incompatible forms of social will, as conceptualised by Ferdinand Tönnies: contractual conventions, societal habits and public opinion. This complex interplay between public opinion and traditional frameworks of habits and contractual relations, as influenced by modern capitalist societies and propelled by digitalisation, profoundly impacts the realisation of publicness in the formation and articulation of public opinion.

Conceptually, the gig public emerges from the profound shifts introduced by the digitised technological environment in the formation of public opinion, situating these changes within a broader sociological framework. Empirically, it thrives on the mutual contractual and habitual adaptation of members of the gig public and their will to visibility, rather than on the free public use of reason envisioned in the Enlightenment normative political-philosophical tradition. It embodies ephemerality, forming around specific issues or events but dissipating once those moments pass.

Reflecting the short-term nature of both stage performances and project-based gig work, the gig public mirrors this transience and fluidity within the realm of public discourse. Engagement within the gig public tends to be spontaneous and loosely structured, often constrained by the difficulty of fostering sustained interaction and in-depth discussion. The participants in these discourses, traditionally conceived of as 'strangers' in public opinion theories, frequently lack established relationships, further complicating the development of collective, enduring public dialogue.

Just as gig workers rely on platforms like Uber, TaskRabbit or Airbnb to mediate and structure their labour, gig publics similarly depend on digital platforms such as Facebook, Twitter, Reddit or TikTok. These platforms not only serve as venues for discourse but also shape its nature by determining what is made visible, how information is disseminated and what types of inter-actions are possible. The gig public thus embodies the dual influence of AI infrastructure, functioning simultaneously as a facilitator of public discourse and a gatekeeper that controls its boundaries and nature, while also reflect-ing the fleeting and ephemeral character of modern public engagement. This represents a significant departure from traditional conceptions of delibera-tion and public opinion formation.

In the contemporary context, the gig public reflects notable structural similarities with gig labour itself. Much like the labour market in the gig economy, characterised by temporary, contract and freelance jobs that lack long-term security or stability and blur the distinction between work and leisure, the gig public embodies an evolving, flexible, temporary, task- or issue-specific and decentralised relationship between individu-als, their private and public lives and digital platforms. This dynamic also reflects the increasing blurring of boundaries between public and private spheres.

Like gig workers, members of gig publics many times operate in uncertain environments where their influence and visibility fluctuate. The attention and engagement that define these publics are transitory, and the exchange of ideas and information is precarious. This instability is compounded by reli-ance on social media platforms that prioritise speed, immediate impact and virality over depth and sustained dialogue, facilitating rapid, yet often super-ficial, exchanges of ideas and opinions and mobilisation around trending top-ics. Such superficial interaction makes it difficult to maintain the depth of discussion required for effecting long-term changes – an essential component of forming a genuine public.

Publicness and the Public Sphere

In the contemporary communified context, we are faced with the challenge of fostering genuine public engagement against a backdrop of transactional relationships and fragmented communications. A path forward requires an analysis of the interplay of social structures, power dynamics, class interests and the nature of technologies developed in this context. This framework directs research to address the key questions of how elite interests manage to dictate narratives and values that impact societal norms and expectations, and how marginalised voices can act against hegemonic narratives to foster authentic democratic discourse. Recognising the habitual and contractual relationships, inherent conflicts and contradictions between social classes and groups – beyond discursive relationships between power elites and the public, such as elite-to-citizen or citizen-to-elite communications – is key to the formation and the understanding of the functioning of the public in the public sphere.

The perspective I propose diverges from the liberal-normative conception of the public sphere, which is often criticised for presuming that public issues with significant, long-term consequences can be deliberated with the general welfare of society in mind, rather than favouring the interests of specific groups. However, I am not advocating for a rejection of this – a kind of synthetic – concept. Rather, I suggest redefining it as a structural-analytical construct, conceptualising the public sphere not as a normative ideal but as a foundational societal 'bowl' in which public communication unfolds – an infrastructure upon, and in relation to which, communicative actions are shaped and enacted.

This reconceptualisation analytically distinguishes between three inter-related concepts: *publicness, the public* and *the public sphere. Publicness* refers to the relational condition in which utterances, actions and affects are made visible, accessible and accountable within a shared space. It structures the conditions under which information, persons or claims enter into collective awareness and deliberation. *The public* emerges as a dynamic network of discursive practices: It is not a fixed or unified subject, but a fluid constellation of individuated actors temporarily oriented around shared concerns, issues or events. These actors are loosely coupled through attention, affect and communication, rather than through permanent association. *The public sphere*, in turn, provides the socio-technical and institutional infrastructure that makes possible the emergence of the public and the circulation of publicness – it organises visibility, structures interaction and modulates access to discourse, participation and recognition. While these three constructs are analytically distinct, they operate in a nested relationship: The public emerges within conditions of publicness, which are themselves contingent upon the infrastructural arrangements of the public sphere.

This tripartite model enables a shift in focus from abstract ideals to empirically grounded analyses of how publics emerge, sustain themselves and disintegrate. Rather than assuming the existence of a stable, coherent public sphere, this framework draws attention to the infrastructural, relational and procedural conditions that make publicness possible and shape the formation of publics. It thus supports a more realistic, context-sensitive understanding of contemporary public life, capable of accounting for fragmentation, asymmetry and evolving media ecologies.

The public sphere as an infrastructure of publicness rests on three main pillars:

1. *Communication Technology, Networks and Media*
    This pillar encompasses the material and technical foundations of public communication, including:

    - Availability and maturity: The extent to which communication technologies are widely accessible and sufficiently developed to support diverse forms of public engagement.
    - Democratic affordances: Features of technology that enable or constrain equal participation, visibility and interaction in public discourse.
    - Mechanisms of access and control: The ownership, governance and regulatory conditions that shape who can use communication technologies, under what terms and with what effects on inclusion and exclusion.

2. *Institutional and Organisational Structures*
    This pillar refers to the formal systems and frameworks that shape public communication, including:

    - Political systems: Legal and normative environments that enable or constrain freedom of expression, media pluralism and content diversity.
    - Economic systems: Ownership models and market dynamics that affect media concentration, platform governance and the commodification of attention and information.
    - Regulatory frameworks: Legal instruments, institutional mechanisms and organisational principles – both national and supranational – that govern media systems and digital platforms.

3. *Communication Culture and Ethical Framework*
    This pillar captures the normative and epistemic conditions under which public discourse takes place, including:

    - Values and norms: Shared cultural beliefs about appropriate forms of public expression, dialogue and engagement.
    - Discursive order: The implicit and explicit rules that guide public interaction – such as standards for truthfulness, civility, argumentation and legitimacy.
    - Epistemic practices: The socially embedded methods for producing, validating and contesting knowledge claims in public discourse, informed by cultural and ethical orientations

By analysing public communication as contingent on this infrastructure, the framework shifts its focus from the normative realm of prescriptive ideals to a structural analysis of empirical and contextual realities. This reconceptuali-sation addresses many of the common criticisms of Habermas' concept of the public sphere, such as its reduction of modern public life to bourgeois ideals, its idealisation of rational discourse, its assumption of a universalistic public interest and its exclusion of power dynamics, gender bias and an overly rigid public/private dichotomy. Instead, the public sphere can be understood as an infrastructure of publicness, akin to J. S. Mill's view of 'publicity': It is a neces-sary condition for publicness – and, by extension, the public – to materialise; however, it provides no guarantee of it.

This perspective invites a nuanced inquiry into how communicative actions are shaped by – and in turn reshape – the underlying societal 'bowl'. A robust public sphere that meets minimal democratic standards – standards that can be empirically assessed – facilitates effective public communication and deliberation. When such a democratically organised infrastructure is in place, it enables the principle of publicness to materialise, enabling publics to communicatively form a collective will.

Publicness is more than an organisational *principle* concerned with individual freedom and public accessibility to rational discussions and decision-making on matters of general interest. In my VARMIL model (Splichal 2022), publicness is conceptualised as both a multidimensional *societal condition* – referring to struc-tural and contextual arrangements, as well as mechanisms of openness, access, visibility, disclosure and recognition – and a *communicative process* – referring to interactive practices of expression, disclosure and discussion through which meaning, recognition and relevance are circulated and contested. Together, these two aspects define a dynamic concept of publicness that asymptotically approaches the public endpoint of the private–public continuum.

Its multidimensionality underscores the relative nature of publicness: not as a fixed or absolute state, but as a composite quality emerging from the interaction of several interdependent dimensions. In this view, instantiations of publicness – such as publics or public opinion – do not exhibit singularly 'more' or 'less' publicness. Rather, each dimension contributes to the charac-ter and degree of publicness within specific societal contexts. It is the combi-nation and configuration of six key dimensions that determine the nature of publicness.

The VARMIL model – an acronym for Visibility, Access, Reflexivity, Mediativity, Influence and Legitimisation – operationalises the concept of publicness through six key dimensions:

- *Visibility*: The reporting of socio-political developments with significant long-term implications, enabling broad awareness, public discussion and opinion formation.

- *Access*: The conditions that enable citizens to access communication channels and public spaces, fostering public reasoning and the development of informed public opinion.
- *Reflexivity*: The capacity of communicative actors to critically evaluate the public relevance of issues, claims and events within the public sphere.
- *Mediativity*: The facilitation of discourse between decision-makers and civil society, contributing to a democratic order of deliberation.
- *Influence*: The capacity of public opinion to shape political and administrative decision-making through institutionalised mechanisms, supporting collective will-formation as a core feature of an 'input-oriented' democracy.
- *Legitimisation*: The requirement for authorities to publicly justify their decisions, enhancing transparency and enabling public oversight to ensure 'output-oriented' political legitimacy.

Each of these six dimensions can be operationalised through specific indicators, allowing for the empirical assessment of the robustness of publicness and the vitality of publics within a democratic framework.

Reimagining publicness and engagement within the gig public requires a thorough understanding of both the opportunities and constraints created by contemporary social and technological developments. The evolution of communication and opinion technologies reflects the ever more influential role of technology in shaping public discourse. While the impact of communication technology has always been significant, albeit contradictory, recent advances in fields such as AI, machine learning and neuroscience are transforming our approaches to knowledge and understanding, leading to unprecedented effects on communication.

The progression of communication technologies demonstrates how each medium not only expands access to information but also restructures public discourse itself. These technologies exhibit significant cognitive and epistemic characteristics by enhancing individual knowledge-making capacities, refining comprehension mechanisms and shaping the processes through which information, knowledge and values are generated, applied and disseminated. AI and machine learning algorithms, for instance, can process vast datasets to identify patterns beyond human perceptual and cognitive limits, driving transformative advancements across diverse fields, including medicine and economics. Similarly, neuroscience technologies – once seen as peripheral to the concerns of social scientists – have recently achieved remarkable precision in brain mapping, deepening our understanding of cognition and opening new pathways for treating mental health conditions.

As these cognitive and epistemic technologies evolve, directly influencing not only their own functions but also their broader societal impacts on decisions and behaviours at both individual and societal levels, they raise important questions about the impact and purpose of content creation, curation and control. The significance of these technologies lies not only in their instrumental capabilities to solve technical problems and accomplish predefined goals but also in their ethical and societal implications. While the distinction between the instrumentality and normative goals of technologies has often been considered external to technology or user-dependent, AI-based epistemic technologies reveal how both the instrumental and critical-reflexive purposes are often integral to the design, with ethical considerations about autonomy, privacy and societal impact embedded within the technology itself. This progression underscores the need to examine how each technology not only impacts communication but also shapes the democratic potential of public engagement and collective opinion formation.

It is essential to approach the communicative pluralism enabled by digitisation and communification critically. Rather than simply accepting it as a genuine virtue of the current information order, we must determine whether it is an 'inevitable byproduct' of technological infrastructure – a byproduct that may ultimately serve to reproduce systems of social surveillance. This cautious framing requires a deeper investigation of how digital infrastructures and algorithmic mediation influence publicness, shaping both the possibilities and limitations of public discourse and collective deliberation.

Outline of the Book

In addressing these concerns, this book offers an initial mapping and critical conceptualisation of the gig public – a concept that captures the fragmented, precarious and performative nature of contemporary public engagement. Drawing parallels to the *gig economy*'s flexible, temporary and insecure employment structures, as well as to *gigging* as a form of public music performance, the gig public reflects how digital tools are reconfiguring the boundaries between personal and public realms. Nowhere is this transformation more evident than on social media platforms, where personal narratives often become public spectacles, further blurring traditional distinctions between private and public domains. The gig public, with its transient, issue-specific, contractual and fragmented characteristics, shows the precarious nature of contemporary civic engagement and challenges traditional conceptions of publicness and collective deliberation.

The core aim of this work is to develop concepts and frameworks that enable us to recognise the interconnections among what have traditionally been seen as disparate concepts. By doing so, it seeks to explore the barriers created by emerging opinion enclaves and societal polarisations, while also addressing the potential to cultivate genuine publics within an inclusive public sphere. The gig public, as conceptualised here, encapsulates both the challenges and opportunities of reinvigorating public discourse in an era shaped by digitalisation, communification and algorithmically mediated interactions.

This work strives to go beyond merely describing the fragmented and transient nature of contemporary public engagement. Instead, it aims to develop the concepts and frameworks necessary for critically examining how to transcend these divisions and establish meaningful connections that foster collective deliberation. In making sense of the contemporary dynamics driving the evolution of publicness, my approach has been to uncover deeper patterns beneath the technological complexity and corporate narratives that dominate today's digital landscape, with the goal of providing a clearer understanding of how publicness can be both reimagined and revitalised in this new paradigm. Rather than getting lost in the vast array of technological details or distracted by corporate rhetoric, the analysis focuses on uncovering the systemic relationships shaping contemporary public engagement. This approach not only helps to clarify how digital platforms influence the nature of publicness but also sheds light on the broader implications for fostering inclusivity and meaningful dialogue within the public sphere.

The book presents a framework for understanding the gig public, exploring its fragmented, episodic and performative characteristics while identifying pathways to transcend these shortcomings. Grounded in critical theory and empirical observation, it provides tools to envision and work towards the formation of genuine publics capable of addressing the complexities of modern society while fostering collective deliberation and meaningful engagement.

Structured in four main parts, the book addresses fundamental questions about gig publics: What is a gig public? Where does a gig public come from? What should we do about gig publics? It critically examines the transformations in the nature of publicness and the public sphere within the context of digitalisation, communification and the growing influence of AI. Divided into four chapters, the study traces the historical evolution of the conceptualisation of publicness, the emergence of new paradigms and strategies to address the challenges of fragmentation in contemporary public life. Situated within a sociological and philosophical framework, it highlights how digital infrastructures, habitual behaviours and contractual relationships impact modern public engagement. It introduces the gig public as a new paradigm, distinct from previous conceptions of publicness due to its reliance on digital platforms, its ephemeral and issue-driven interactions, and its susceptibility to the algorithmically curated structures that shape modern communication.

Chapter 1 explores the origins of the gig public by tracing the historical and conceptual evolution of publicness. It begins with an exploration of early twentieth-century sociological efforts to conceptualise the public by integrating normative politico-philosophical ideas stemming from the Enlightenment. These early sociological perspectives on the public and public opinion are contrasted with the emergence of the 'public sphere' concept, a framework that marked a significant departure in understanding the collective public use of reason. While I critique the concept of the public sphere as inconsistent and biased compared to earlier sociological conceptualisations, I argue that critically examining its assumptions, recognising its implications and exploring alternative approaches to creating and conceptualising publicness are crucial intellectual tasks.

Building on these premises, the chapter investigates the circumstances surrounding the introduction of the term 'public sphere' in discussions of publicness, examining its implications and highlighting the significance of shared epistemic spaces where individuals engage in reasoning and deliberation. It then turns to exploring the largely Internet-driven dispersion of discursive identities, with particular attention paid to the emergence of 'counterpublics' and their *entitativity* – the processes via which cohesive identities are formed within these fragmented and oppositional 'publics'. The final section examines how digital distractions embedded in social media platforms – such as multitasking, constant notifications and algorithmically curated content – impede our ability to filter meaningful information from noise. These distractions foster exclusive interpretations and misunderstandings, ultimately intensifying the technologically driven fragmentation of online discursive interactions. Through this lens, Chapter 1 establishes the foundational context for understanding how the gig public emerges within these fractured and digitally mediated landscapes, setting the stage for a deeper exploration of its characteristics and implications in the following chapter.

Chapter 2 focuses on the relationship between the gig public, customised habits and contractual behaviour within a *communified* and AI-driven environment, tracing the transition from the elitist model of the (bourgeois) public to the emergence of gig publics. It explores the evolution of the conceptualisation and formation of publics and public opinion, revealing the increasing yet often overlooked influence of habitual and contractual dynamics in shaping public discourse in the digital age.

The chapter begins with a sociological critique of the Enlightenment's idealised normative vision of rational public discourse, contrasting these lofty aspirations with sociological observations of real-world group behaviour, which often falls short of the Enlightenment ideals. It then explores the habitual and customary aspects of public opinion formation, illustrating how collective attitudes are impacted by ingrained social habits and routines. The final section focuses on the evolution of the formation of publics through habitual and contractual relations, highlighting the shift from traditional media to digital platforms, where corporate-controlled algorithms now dominate engagement, potentially undermining authentic participatory engagement.

Chapter 3 examines how the rise of the *attention economy* (Simon 1971) and the *intention economy* (Searls 2012), within the broader framework of *surveillance capitalism* (Zuboff 2019), is reshaping the boundaries between the public and private spheres on the Internet. It focuses on the evolving contractual relationships between platform owners, content creators, service providers and how these are changing the dynamics of public and private interactions. By exploring the interplay between ephemeral engagements and deeper structural forces, the chapter highlights the role of gig publics as both products of and responses to the changing nature of contemporary publicness.

The first section explores the shift from traditional forms of publicness, where individuals engage in socially structured discourse, to the *performativisation of publicness*, driven by the will to visibility and self-presentation. This shift is exemplified by practices such as using mobile phone cameras to document actions and transform them into 'public events'. Social media platforms encourage spectacle and self-promotion, fostering performative actions or utterances through which something is 'performed into existence' or 'brought into being'. By prioritising visibility over deliberation and presence over reasoned discourse, they fundamentally alter the nature of public participation.

The chapter's central focus is on gig publics, which blur the traditional boundaries between public and private spheres. Unlike traditional newspaper-reading publics, gig publics are characterised by fleeting attention, task-based interactions and the superficial nature of digital discourse shaped by algorithms and the transactional logic of the gig economy. AI-driven systems prioritise convenience through habitual and contractual behaviours, infantilising users and limiting their autonomy, thus preventing the development of an informed and reflexive public.

The book concludes by posing critical questions about whether fragmented gig publics can foster collective deliberation despite their inherent structural limitations. *Chapter 4* explores potential opportunities and emergent strategies to counteract the growing fragmentation of modern public life, offering a roadmap for reimagining publicness in the digital age. I propose actionable strategies to revitalise inclusivity and deliberation, alongside efforts to liberate the public sphere from the corporate takeover.

The concluding chapter advocates for digital literacy programmes to equip individuals with the critical skills needed to navigate effectively and engage responsibly in virtual spaces. It also calls for greater accountability from digital platforms, emphasising the need for transparent algorithms and moderation policies that actively promote diversity, reduce bias and foster a more inclusive online environment. Recognising the persistent issue of the digital divide, the chapter stresses the importance of ensuring equitable access to digital platforms and resources to bridge gaps in participation and representation across different social and geographical contexts. To counteract the transient and superficial nature of gig publics, it suggests mechanisms that encourage more sustained engagement and depth in online discussions.

These normative interventions, however, must be understood within the broader context of deep structural and epistemic transformations that digitalisation and platformisation have introduced into public life. The blurring of boundaries between the public and the private, and between the authentic and the synthetic, as manifested in the gig public, challenges traditional notions of privacy, identity and publicness. Driven by AI technologies and the surveillance economy, these transformations not only call into question our fundamental concepts of privacy, publicness and authenticity, but also redefine the very nature of public engagement itself. They shift it away from the structured, deliberative processes envisioned by the Enlightenment thinkers towards more fragmented and transient exchanges, where attention is fleeting and engagement is often shaped by algorithmic incentives rather than meaningful discourse.

These reconfigurations prompt a re-evaluation of how we connect, deliberate and form collective opinions in an increasingly communified and commodified world. This study critically examines the implications of these changes, exploring how the rise of gig publics challenges traditional conceptions of publicness and public discourse. It seeks to understand not only the technological forces at play but also the societal, cultural and political consequences of these transformations. By analysing historical shifts and contradictions, the study sheds light on the tensions between the democratising potential of AI-driven communication platforms and the risks of fragmentation, surveillance and exploitation inherent in the surveillance economy.

Through this examination, the study provides a framework for rethinking, reclaiming and reinventing publicness, while exploring pathways to foster more inclusive, equitable and meaningful public discourse and collective democratic action in an era of algorithmic governmentality.

Chapter 1

FROM COLLECTIVE TO COUNTER

Understanding the Evolving Territories of Publicness

This chapter raises a critical question about the shifting nature of publicness, particularly the movement from traditional collective identities to the proliferation of fragmented and diversified publics in contemporary society. It invites readers to reflect on the challenges posed by this fragmentation, including the reconfiguration of public spheres, and to explore the conceptual origins and implications of these evolving forms of public engagement.

Crowds, Publics, Public Opinion and the Public Sphere

From social norms to epistemic contracts in conceptualising the public

This section explores how early twentieth-century sociological theorists sought to conceptualise the public as a distinct form of collective behaviour, integrating normative ideals inherited from Enlightenment political philosophy with emerging insights into conformity to social norms, the role of the press in shaping public discourse and the mechanisms through which shared knowledge and beliefs are socially coordinated. Special attention is given to the ethical principles associated with the concept of the general will, as well as to the structural conditions and social forces that shape the emergence and coherence of publics.

The public sphere – the return of public reasoning

The emergence of the concept of the *public sphere* marks a conceptual shift in how collective public discourse is understood, moving beyond traditional notions of *the public* and *public opinion*. This section investigates the historical context in which the term gained prominence and highlights its implications for imagining shared spaces in which individuals are expected to engage in reasoned deliberation.

The Fragmentation of Discursive Identities and Identity Discourses

From proletarian to self-enclosed counterpublics

This section traces the conceptual evolution from proletarian publics to self-enclosed 'counterpublics', focusing on the changing nature and composition of publics over time. It explores the emergence of the concept of counter-publics as spaces of resistance and examines how their dynamics have been reconfigured in contemporary discourse.

The entitativity of counterpublics

This section analyses the *entitativity* – the degree of coherence and identity – within 'counterpublics'. It explores how shared identities form within fragmented discursive spaces and examines the internal dynamics that sustain these collectivities.

Technology-driven fragmentation of discursive interaction

This section examines how digital distractions – such as multitasking, constant notifications and algorithmically curated content – undermine the quality of online discourse. These factors contribute to a growing inability to distinguish between signal and noise, fostering divergent interpretations and misunderstandings that further fragment discursive interactions in digital environments.

* * *

Crowds, Publics, Public Opinion and the Public Sphere

The Enlightenment placed the concepts of the public and publicness (then known as 'publicity') at the core of debates about political freedom, justice and democratic governance. These ideas were central to the normative political writings of Enlightenment thinkers, who conceptualised them as instruments for controlling political power and as criteria for rightful action. Yet, despite their philosophical significance, they remained underdeveloped within the social sciences and played only a marginal role in classical sociology. This began to change in the late nineteenth and early twentieth centuries, when influential theorists such as Gabriel Tarde, Ferdinand Tönnies, Robert Park and the Chicago School sociologists engaged more deeply with these concepts, laying the groundwork for their integration into social theory. In the 1920s, Walter Lippmann and John Dewey further advanced the discourse in the United States, debating whether the public was an illusory construct or a substantive social actor.

These scholars marked a significant departure from earlier sociological thought, in which publicness was largely overlooked. They redefined the public as a fluid and dynamic entity, in contrast to earlier static, normative conceptualisations and the notion of stable, cohesive traditional groups governing collective behaviour. At the same time, sociological analyses of the public and public opinion contributed to a critical de-idealisation of the normative ideals embedded in Enlightenment politico-philosophical theories.

Reflecting a shift to a more flexible and evolving understanding of social interactions, the public came to be seen as shaped by diverse individual and collective experiences and relationships, rather than by rigid customs and norms. The introduction of the idea of the general or common will, borrowed from political philosophy, signalled a significant departure from a purely interactionist perspective in sociology by underscoring the importance of collective traditions, customs and norms in shaping social life.

Although these sociological reflections on the public found notable successors, including Theodor Adorno, Herbert Blumer, C. Wright Mills and Pierre Bourdieu, this perspective gradually lost prominence in mainstream sociology and opinion polling. In the decades that followed, these earlier insights were largely overlooked in administrative opinion research as well as in the critical conceptualisation of the 'public sphere'. In opinion polling, this neglect contributed to the underestimation of the collective and interactive dynamics involved in the formation of public opinion. Meanwhile, the rational-critical tradition of the public sphere that later emerged tended to disregard the influence of interest-driven hierarchies and structural inequalities in shaping communicative actions within class-stratified societies.

During the period dominated by the concept of the 'public sphere', only Dewey and Lippmann retained significant influence – mainly because they championed freedom of expression and academic freedom while also engaging with a wide range of social issues extending beyond publicness, covering topics from journalism and the press to psychology, education, democracy and international politics.

Nevertheless, the early critical sociological insights into the complex fabric of publics and public opinion, developed a century ago, may be even more relevant today, in light of rising inequalities, increasing political polarisation and the erosion of political communication culture.

From social norms to epistemic contracts in conceptualising the public

The roots of the sociological conceptualisation of the public, as proposed by Park and Tönnies, are deeply embedded in the politico-philosophical tradition of the Enlightenment. Their conceptualisations of the public draw on the ethical foundations of the Enlightenment concept of the *general will* (*Gesamtwille*). Both sociologists draw on ideas developed by philosophers ranging from Hobbes, Locke and Rousseau to Kant, Fichte and Hegel, highlighting the evolving concept of collective will and its significance for public life. While their perspectives offer valuable sociological insights into the phenomenon of the public, their contributions were unfortunately marginalised during the twentieth century in both administrative and critical research on public opinion and the public sphere.

Both Park and Tönnies sought to clearly delineate the public within theoretical frameworks, while also examining its role in the complex dynamics of social life through empirical analysis. A central feature of their approaches is the emphasis on collective self-consciousness, which emerges within collectivities and stands in contrast to individual self-consciousness. They distinguish between two types of collectivities: one in which the collective will subsumes individual minds, thereby reducing personal individuality, and another in which individuals actively engage their rational faculties to participate in public discourse, resolve differences and shape a shared collective will.

In Park's analysis, this distinction lies in the difference between *crowd* and *public*, both of which are temporary, unstructured groups. A crowd is a large group that spontaneously gathers and is unified by a shared purpose, such as attending an event or participating in a demonstration. In contrast, the public is a dispersed group engaged in discussions on public issues, often facilitated by the mass media. For Tönnies, the distinctions in framing collective will in social organisation are encapsulated by the concepts of *Gemeinschaft* and *Gesellschaft*. *Gemeinschaft* emphasises personal and communal bonds formed through customs or religion, while *Gesellschaft* is characterised by impersonal, rationalised relationships driven by economic, legal and ethical principles. Within *Gesellschaft*, public opinion becomes one of the basic 'complex forms of social will', along with the economy and legislation, that collectively shape social organisation.

Both Park and Tönnies engage with the Enlightenment notion of the general will, viewing it as the collective cognitive basis of group behaviour. They oppose the tendency to consider public opinion merely as the sum total of vaguely articulated opinions on any matter – a perspective that later prevailed among proponents of polling. However, they differ in how they apply this concept to conceptualise the public and its role in society.

Crowd and *public* are fundamental concepts in the study of collective behaviour introduced by Robert Park, a founder of the 'Chicago School' of sociology. These concepts were earlier developed by Gabriel Tarde within the French scholarly tradition, although Park appears to have been unaware of Tarde's contributions. Drawing on the notion of the general will from political philosophy, Park distinguishes the public from both the stable normative order and the collective behaviour manifested in the supra-individual nature of tradition, custom and norm, as well as from all other social groups. He emphasises dynamic social interactions within urban settings, suggesting that the public and public opinion are formed in a fluid process of generating collective will, shaped by diverse experiences and relationships. This collective will, as Park views it, is more adaptable and context-driven than the more fixed and abstract notion of the general will.

Both the public and its counterpart – the crowd – are considered 'psychological products' that stand in opposition to normative societal structures. They are transient, extra-institutional entities dominated by a form of collective will that does not manifest as a norm and thus cannot be equated with the general will. These formations enable the creation of new social connections by drawing individuals away from pre-existing ties and groups based on shared norms, traditions and culture.

Although crowds and publics, unlike traditional groups, lack established customs or traditions, they can nonetheless play an important role in generating new ones. While both induce social change, they do so through distinct mechanisms: Crowds operate via emotional contagion and the suppression of differences, whereas publics engage at a relatively rational level of discourse – 'in the sense that it is *critical*; meaning that what has been said may be questioned, *negated* and *contradicted*', and done so without fear of societal domination inhibiting dialogue (Gouldner 1976, 98).

Influenced by the ideas of Fichte and Hegel, Park (1904) conceptualised the public as striving to assess individual opinions from a standpoint that transcends personal perspectives – even though it never fully attains this 'supra-individual' point of view. Unlike a crowd, which can exhibit chaotic and emotionally charged dynamics, the public functions through more intricate interactions that promote individual thinking, the exchange of well-considered opposing views and the inclusion of diverse perspectives rooted in tradition. This understanding highlights the dynamic nature of public opinion, which emerges from critical individual attitudes and is neither uniformly understood nor universally accepted. Public opinion is not merely the sum of individual viewpoints or a consensus of agreed-upon beliefs; rather, it exists as something external to any single individual, expressed in varying ways by different people. This divergence from personal perspectives often leads to public opinion being perceived as an objective phenomenon. However, because the transient impulses and interests of individuals tend to overshadow customary and moral commonalities, the public – unlike more cohesive traditional groups – lacks the capacity for sustained collective action.

Central to Park's concept of the public are the ideas of *opposition* and *reciprocity*, which he understands as psychological contracts that contribute to social differentiation. In society, reciprocal interests are represented by opposing entities that define and constrain one another. Typical examples include the relationships between rulers and subjects, teachers and pupils, buyers and sellers or political parties. In each case, one side presupposes the existence of the other, and neither can be fully understood in isolation. Both attain self-consciousness through their opposition to other individuals or collectivities. The same dynamic applies to the public, where divergent opinions from different individuals come into conflict, clarify one another and collectively contribute to the formation of public consciousness.

This means that public opinion is neither universally shared nor uniformly accepted by all individuals within the public, and it varies in how it is expressed across different people. As a result, even when grounded in reasoned deliberation, public opinion does not establish norms. Unlike laws, which are rooted in a mental framework called the 'general will', public opinion reflects only a portion of the fluctuating psychological conditions of a social group – the public. Often, it amounts to little more than a naïve collective impulse, easily influenced or manipulated, suggesting that the public operates at a similar stage of consciousness development as the crowd.

This observation indicates that the crowd and the public – one emerging from similarities, the other from difference – are not mutually exclusive. Rather, they share overlapping characteristics and, as Tarde noted, can transform into one another. Still, Park did not explicitly address the specific social conditions that give rise to one form of collectivity over the other.

While Park was primarily concerned with two key forms of collective behaviour – the crowd and the public – Tönnies' sociological agenda focused on the *forms of social will* characteristic of *Gemeinschaft* (community) and *Gesellschaft* (society) as fundamental drivers of social dynamics and public life, from feudal to capitalist and socialist societies. His theory captures the long-term transformations and underlying tensions between intimate, affective communal bonds and the more impersonal, rational associations that define modern social life.

Building on his philosophical predecessors, Tönnies incorporated public opinion into his theory of social will as one of the dominant complex forms of social will in the *Gesellschaft*-type social structure. Public opinion reflects the collective moral and ethical dimensions of public behaviour, shaped by the public and takes on various forms depending on social contexts and historical periods. Tönnies thus distinguishes 'public opinion' – seen as a conglomerate of diverse and sometimes conflicting views, wishes and intentions – from 'Public Opinion', which represents the unified opinion of the public. This unified force is not merely an expression of a common will but *'the most intellectual expression of the same common will that is also reflected in convention and legislation*. Its subject, which aligns with society and the state as the subjects of the latter, may therefore be defined as "the public"' (Tönnies 1922, 77; emphasis added).

Within *Gesellschaft*, public opinion represents the third complex form of social will, alongside *convention*, which underpins the economy and civil society, and *state legislation*, which regulates behaviour through a rational-legal order. In contrast to the traditional, emotive or absolutist qualities of the 'natural will' (*Wesenwille*), which are rooted in emotions, habits, beliefs, custom and religion, public opinion is a complex form of collective 'reflexive will' (*Kürwille*). Reflexive will arises from artificial, deliberate and conscious acts, in which the means and ends are clearly distinguished. The key difference between these two forms of will lies in their relation to thought: Natural will includes an element of unreflexive, instinctive thought, whereas reflexive will is embedded within a conscious process of reasoning that involves freedom, deliberation and rational choice.

This distinction is also reflected in the evolving relationships between the individual and the social, as well as between will and reasoning. In a community, 'the general is prius, and the specific and the private is posterius', whereas in society, the reverse is true: the specific precedes the general (Tönnies 1922, 23). While natural will shapes thought, the opposite holds for reflexive will: consciousness becomes liberated, allowing thinking to dictate the will.

Tönnies' structural focus offers a broader, materialist understanding of how and why public opinion forms, compared to earlier normative theories. By centring on class and social structure, he highlights the social factors and power dynamics that shape the formation of publics and public opinion. His emphasis on social structure and collective will provides a more subtle interpretation of public opinion as a product of deeper social dynamics, rather than merely individual actions or media influence. Unlike early democratic theorists who viewed public opinion as a straightforward expression of the will of the people, Tönnies recognises its limitations and dangers: While public opinion has the potential to be a powerful force for change, it is also highly susceptible to manipulation by ruling elites and the press.

Tönnies emphasises that opinions often reflect the underlying interests of different social categories and classes, suggesting that similar opinions reveal shared interests, while conflicts of opinion may be understood as struggles over resources, status and power. His empirical sociological perspective highlights the influence of socio-economic factors – such as occupation, living conditions, urbanisation, class affiliation, social status, property, education, religion and gender – in shaping individual opinions and the resulting tensions that emerge between groups with divergent interests. The most profound division in opining, according to Tönnies, is 'between the owning and therefore ruling class and the propertyless and therefore dominated class, between upper and lower, masters and servants, rich and poor, between "capital" and labour' (Tönnies 1922, 114, 118–121). While opinions on specific issues may vary, and the alignment of opinion groups may shift, the fundamental opposition between the ruling bourgeois class and the proletariat persists, with each group's opinions rooted in their material interests.

In a more optimistic, future-oriented perspective, Tönnies argues that the development of opining is chiefly a result of advancements in scientific knowledge. This is especially the case with public opinion, which primarily relates to public affairs: 'Public opinion's main activity is criticism, arising from dissatisfaction with existing governments, traditional conditions and prevailing religious doctrines. Initially, this dissatisfaction is emotional, but over time, it becomes more thoughtful and insightful; initially silent and vague, it gradually grows louder and clearer; initially scattered and powerless, it eventually becomes coherent and organized' (ibid., 121).

The sociological perspectives introduced by Tönnies and Park marked an important shift by moving the focus away from emotional contagion and the suppression of individual critical abilities within crowds to a more nuanced understanding of societal dynamics. However, they lack a robust analysis of democratic mechanisms – such as parliaments, courts or public forums – that could facilitate conflict resolution and consensus-building. By invoking the concept of the general will, their discussion highlights the importance of collective traditions, customs and norms, suggesting that a purely interactionist approach may overlook the deeper structural influences shaping social life and informing collective decision-making processes. Public opinion is recognised as holding the potential to foster democratic engagement, as are the collective forces of social will – tied to deeper traditions, norms, power structures and class interests – that can manipulate it.

This balanced perspective avoids the utopianism of later theories that idealise the potential for rational discourse while neglecting the structural forces shaping public behaviour (e.g., Habermas), as well as the dystopian view that focuses solely on the negative aspects of media influence and regards public opinion as a product of mass deception (e.g., the Frankfurt School, Arendt).

The public sphere – the return of public reasoning

The flourishing era of sociological inquiry into public opinion largely ended before the Second World War, leading to a notable decline in sociological engagement with the concepts of the public and public opinion. This shift occurred as the field became increasingly dominated by the rise of polling techniques and the development of political propaganda, which overshadowed theoretical explorations of publicness. The crisis in the sociological understanding of the concept of the public persists to this day. As Lasswell (1957, 33–34) noted, despite considerable methodological advances in twentieth-century public opinion research, '[a]t the level of fundamental theory nothing has been added' Similarly, Parsons (1963, 37) observed that 'the development of research technology in the field of opinion and attitude study has outrun the development of theory'. Even later attempts to 'redress the balance by essaying a contribution in the theoretical area' continued to prioritise a conceptualisation of 'public opinion' not as a dynamic process of public opining, but as a product of influence – 'a way of having an effect on the attitudes and opinions of others through intentional (though not necessarily rational) action' (Parsons 1963, 38).

Parsons' attempt to theoretically rehabilitate public opinion as a significant form of *influence*, rather than an instance of *publicness*, met with little success. Sociological appeals to public opinion continued yet were often perceived as either 'voices crying in the wilderness' or 'smoke screens masking the egotistic aspirations of this or that "pressure group"'. Instead of one genuine public opinion, we have thousands of pseudo-public opinions of factions, sects and individuals' (Sorokin 1941/1992, 135). Public opinion remained a descriptive term associated with the propaganda and polling technologies employed in opinion and attitude research. It was viewed as a component of 'automatic control mechanisms' designed to minimise 'the disorganization present in all complex social systems' (Parsons 1942, 563–564). This association of public opinion with (research on) communication effects, persuasion, attitude formation and voting intentions shifted the focus of public opinion studies towards its role as an agent of control, helping to maintain social stability within complex societies.

Subsequent theories, such as those of Habermas, while reaffirming the Enlightenment-rooted ideal of publicness, focus on rational discourse in the public sphere but often overlook the structural forces and behavioural dynamics that shape social groups. The marginalisation of earlier sociological contributions to the study of the public and public opinion after the 1930s reflects a troubling disciplinary shift towards opinion polling and administrative research, privileging quantitative methods over deeper sociological analysis. This methodological turn has contributed to the neglect of critical frameworks that could provide richer insights into the complexities of social interaction and collective behaviour. Despite ongoing critiques that polling methodologies risk obscuring these richer conceptual dimensions, foundational sociological theories remain largely overlooked and underutilised.

The introduction of the 'public sphere' into Anglo-American social theory and empirical research – spurred by the 1989 English translation of Habermas' *The Structural Transformation of the Public Sphere* – marked a turning point. While this work reignited interest in Enlightenment politico-philosophical ideas about publicness, it inadvertently contributed to the marginalisation of a rich sociological tradition in public opinion theory and research. As the critical epistemic value of public opinion declined, the public – once its central harbinger – was displaced from its pivotal role, a position it has not regained within public sphere theory. With the rise of the public sphere concept, both the public and public opinion failed to reemerge from the theoretical ashes as central elements in theoretical discussions. Unlike scholars like Parsons, who sought to reintroduce public opinion into sociological theory, or contemporary researchers leveraging AI to shape online opinion and behaviour, public sphere theory has largely sidelined the processes through which publics are formed and public opinion is expressed.

The introduction of the term 'public sphere', coined half a century ago as a translation of the German word *Öffentlichkeit*, sparked critical interest by marking a significant departure from the established English terms 'public opinion' and 'the public', which had fallen out of favour in critical theory. Although *Öffentlichkeit* has been used in German for over two centuries, it had traditionally been translated into English as 'publicity' and 'the public' – terms that are not true semantic equivalents of *Öffentlichkeit*. Given the centrality of *Öffentlichkeit* in Habermas' book, the translator faced the challenge of finding a more appropriate English rendering. The phrase 'the public sphere' was chosen as a solution, but it has proven to be an inconsistent and problematic choice. Unfortunately, the assumption that 'public sphere' and *Öffentlichkeit* are semantically equivalent is widespread among English-speaking scholars. This unresolved terminological issue continues to shape English-language debates in the public sphere, often resulting in overly simplistic conceptualisations.

The discomfort with the term *Öffentlichkeit* among non-German scholars dates back to the early twentieth century, as evidenced by the doctoral dissertation of the prominent American sociologist Robert Park. Although he conducted his research in Germany and defended his dissertation *Masse und Publikum* (1904) in German, he chose not to use the already widely accepted term *Öffentlichkeit* when discussing phenomena such as *öffentliche Meinung* (public opinion) and *öffentliche Versammlungen* (public gatherings), which were more comprehensible to non-German readers and more readily translatable to English. While the German term *Öffentlichkeit* had not yet been coined at the time of Kant's seminal exploration of the principle of publicness – referred to by Kant (1795/1939) as *Publicität*, later *Publizität* in German, as equivalent to the English term 'publicity' – Hegel (1821/2001) had already incorporated the more abstract notion of *Öffentlichkeit* into his study of (public) law, the state and public opinion. Despite its subsequent centrality in these debates in Germany, Park notably refrained from using the term.

A particular challenge with the concept of *Öffentlichkeit* is its bivalence between the normative and the empirical, or between the abstract and the concrete. *Öffentlichkeit / Publicness* serves as the supreme principle of democratic action (Kant) and value-rational organisation (Weber), forming part of the basic constitutional provisions of democracies. Normatively, *Öffentlichkeit* connects and mediates between justice, legality and reason, reconciling politics as coercive action with the moral foundation of democratic association: 'All actions that affect the rights of other men are wrong if their maxim is not consistent with publicness' (Kant 1795/1939).

Beyond this normative role, *Öffentlichkeit* also has a descriptive meaning, though this is relatively loose and vague. On the one hand, it refers to the circulated opinions of citizens in society; on the other, to a loosely defined collective body, ideally sovereign over political decisions. The 'principle of publicity' implied not only the right of individuals to publish their opinions but also the right to be informed about matters vital to citizens' lives and to exercise control over political decision-making bodies. Within this framework, public opinion is viewed as a quintessential social-communicative phenomenon of historical significance, facilitated by communication technologies and representing a complex manifestation of societal will, as espoused by Tönnies (1922).

The concept of publicness did not emerge arbitrarily; rather, it was a deliberate outcome shaped by historical forces, including technological advancements. The Enlightenment era marked the rise of publicness, driven largely by the transformative impact of printing technology. This breakthrough created the physical infrastructure – pamphlets, books, newspapers – that enabled both individual expression and the widespread dissemination of opinions, laying the groundwork for public opinion as a central socio-communicative phenomenon.

In the 1930s, a new technological innovation – opinion polling – disrupted prevailing understandings of public opinion. While printing technology empowered public debate by amplifying voices, the epistemic software of polling introduced systematic methods to measure and aggregate private opinions as survey response data. By producing data-driven representations of 'the public,' polling fundamentally reconfigured the understanding of public opinion – shifting it from a deliberative, discursive process to a statistical construct that increasingly guided political decisions and media narratives.

The Fragmentation of Discursive Identities and Identity Discourses

Even more than six decades since its original German publication in 1962, Habermas' *Structural Transformation*, together with his subsequent works, retains its profound richness and influence across several academic disciplines. The English translation of Habermas' work (1989) coincided not only with the rise of personal computers and the Internet but also with a significant social upheaval, marked by the fall of communist systems. These unprecedented revolutionary developments triggered renewed interest in age-old questions about the democratic affordances of publicness, thus making Habermas' work particularly relevant during these critical times for the revival of publicness, the public and the public sphere.

Few books from the second half of the twentieth century have been subject to such comprehensive scrutiny across diverse academic disciplines as *Structural Transformation*, which remains a catalyst for constructive debates on topics like public life, civil society and the future of democracy. Yet, it also incites strong and persistent criticism that fosters in-depth discussions and provides new valuable insights. Among the criticisms of the theory of the public sphere, which point out the peculiarities and limitations of this conceptual invention (Splichal 1981; Marx Ferree et al. 2002; Aubin 2014; O'Mahony 2021), two orientations are especially relevant, albeit not always fully justified: criticising (1) the separation of the 'public sphere' from the classical sociological concepts 'the public' and 'public opinion' and (2) its conceptualisation beyond the materiality of work and production, without recognising the interplay of communication, technology, materiality and production relations. A third line of criticism – politico-historical in nature – is less relevant to our analysis here. This critique argues (Boyle 2012) that Habermas' historical account in *The Structural Transformation*, which describes the politically functioning bourgeois public (sphere) as a dialectical progression in the nineteenth century, is historically inaccurate for both Germany and other European countries.

While the term 'public sphere' gained prominence with the translation of Habermas' book, its intellectual roots, which Habermas may not have recognised, can be traced back to Marx's conception of the press as a 'third element' *mediating* between those in power and civil society. In fact, from the outset, the ideas of 'publicity' and 'the public' have emphasised the important role of the press (and later other media) in democratic societies, which have retained their central role in the 'mediated public sphere'.

In his early works, Marx (1842) maintained an idealistic vision of the press as a platform – 'the third element' – where rulers and the ruled, not as individuals but as 'intellectual forces' embodying reason transcending their narrow interests, could engage in mutual *critique* of each other's principles and demands – free from the 'interference' of public opinion and publics, which were not part of Marx's conceptualisation of the third element. Yet, alongside this notion of the press as an abstract, disinterested intermediary, Marx also emphasised its capacity for *(self-)reflection*. He described the press as a 'speech bond' that connects people and as 'the most general way by which individuals can communicate their intellectual being. [...] What I cannot be for others, I am not and cannot be for myself' (ibid.). For Marx, the press could fulfil its *mediatory* and *reflexive* role only if it operated independently of *market laws* and was not subordinated to *entrepreneurial freedom*.

In contrast to Marx, a defining feature of Habermas' later conceptualisation of publicness and the public sphere is its lack of materialist foundations. While late nineteenth- and early twentieth-century critical theorists – building on Marx's framework – analysed how political, economic and technological transformations eroded the intrinsic autonomy of the public, public opinion and the media, Habermas explicitly rejected Marx's emphasis on labour and modes of production as the primary forces driving economic development and human progress. Instead, his idealisation of the Enlightenment project, grounded in Kantian conceptions of publicness, reveals an optimistic faith in rational discourse and democratic deliberation. This theoretical orientation aligns with a growing emphasis on politically correct communication norms, often accompanied by a diminished commitment to working-class rights.

Yet this perspective overlooked the insights from the sociological tradition that critically examines the conditions, complexities and limits of these ideals. Scholars like Gabriel Tarde, Ferdinand Tönnies, Robert Park, John Dewey and C. Wright Mills provided a critical lens on modernity, pointing to the roles of power, culture and social structure. Their works challenge the assumption that rational discourse alone can bring about a just society and highlight the importance of situating public reasoning within its broader historical and social contexts.

While overshadowing a substantial sociological tradition of the late nineteenth and early twentieth centuries, Habermas' idealised vision of the public sphere has generated a broad spectrum of both affirmative and critical responses in the social sciences. This has contributed to the widespread acceptance of the public sphere as a fundamental concept in academic discourse – though it is often trivialised when reduced to a mere synonym for the print and electronic media through which news and opinions circulate.

This conceptual recognition has also spurred numerous innovative modifications, as evidenced by the proliferation of adjectival qualifiers seeking to characterise both 'the public sphere' and 'the public'. These modifiers encompass a wide range of descriptors, including strong and weak; micro and global; rational and affective; issue-specific; proletarian and subaltern; alternative, emancipatory and democratic; inclusive, participatory and collaborative; engaged, empowered and pluralistic; agonistic, responsive and accountable; and mediated, networked and online, as well as virtual, hashtag and digital publics and/or public spheres.

Dewey (1927/1946, 107) cautioned that the greatest challenge to democratisation lies not in the absence of the public but in the existence of *too many* publics. This proliferation, he argued, obstructs the identification of key social issues that warrant collective deliberation, resulting in what Sorokin (1941/1992, p. 135) termed 'thousands of pseudo-public opinions'. Likewise, the expanding lexicon of adjectives used to qualify the public sphere complicates efforts to define its core characteristics.

The enthusiasm to reconceptualise the public sphere has only intensified with the transnationalisation and globalisation of communication. These developments have foregrounded the challenge of establishing a 'transnational public sphere' and cultivating 'transnational publics' – further diluting the capacity of publics and public opinion to shape political decision-making (Splichal 2012).

These adjectives, each highlighting distinct aspects and developments of the public sphere and publics across various social contexts, reflect a spectrum of normative and analytical perspectives. They can also signify gradations of intensity and comparative distinctions – such as differentiating between *weak(est)* and *strong(est)* publics. Furthermore, they imply the coexistence of contrasting forms, whether as products of historical evolution (e.g., the shift from weak to *strong(er)* publics) or as idealised typologies (e.g., weak *versus* strong publics).

The expansion of empirical research has intensified the tension between two conceptual approaches: the original normative, theoretically pure notion of publicness rooted in political philosophy and more recent descriptive conceptions of the public sphere, which are often vague, arbitrary and increasingly treated as boundary objects across various scientific disciplines. While this growing conceptual ambiguity may foster interdisciplinary dialogue and bridge theory with practice, it does so at the expense of conceptual clarity, critical epistemic value and practical relevance – ultimately diluting the ana-lytical power of publicness and the public sphere as scholarly constructs.

The proliferation of adjective modifiers in rebranding 'the public (sphere)', effectively multiplying its conceptual iterations, has obscured the inherent nature of publicness. The renaming and (implied) reconceptualisation of a core theoretical concept, as the public sphere no doubt represents, carries profound implications that extend beyond the realms of theory and episte-mology, with significant practical repercussions for those potentially involved and those excluded from the public sphere.

An emblematic example of the consequences of such renaming is elo-quently presented by Galbraith (2006) in his critique of how professional dis-course replaced 'capitalism' and 'capitalists' with 'market system' and 'market forces'. This lexical shift creates the illusion of impersonal market dynam-ics operating like an 'invisible hand', thereby obscuring wealth's structural role in economic and social systems. The depersonalisation of capitalism and functional anonymisation of capitalists – removing them from public scrutiny – ultimately reinforces capital owners' interests.

Likewise, the conceptual erasure of the public and public opinion from pre-vailing notions of the public sphere creates the illusion of its all-inclusiveness while obscuring its structural dependence on dominant economic and politi-cal interests. This renders the public sphere an elusive construct that mystifies actual relations of communicative power, privileging liberal normative ideals over substantive democratic engagement (Browne 2018, 9). Such conceptual framing not only impedes the identification of historical constraints on mean-ingful democratic participation but also diverts attention from urgent public matters with profound societal consequences – including entrenched inequal-ity, political destabilisation and resurgent authoritarian threats.

Much contemporary scholarship employs public sphere modifiers that implicitly reinforce its reduction to purely discursive dimensions. Ironically, this persists even in *technologically* specific qualifiers – *digital, networked, algo-rithmic, hashtag or datafied* – of the public sphere and publics, which dominate empirical research focused on the Internet and social media. Although digiti-sation is clearly a technology-driven development with significant economic and political implications – fuelling surveillance capitalism and potentially undermining democratic politics via the privatisation and monopolisation of digital platform ownership and the management – most empirical studies of 'the digital public sphere' remain narrowly focused on discursive patterns, systematically neglecting these structural power dimensions.

The fundamental paradox of 'networked publics' and similar techno-logically 'modified' public spheres lies in how their technological framing obscures their most consequential transformation: becoming *privately* owned by 'surveillance capitalists'. As Zuboff demonstrates, 'our visibility is magnified and compelled not only by the public-ness of networked spaces but by the fact that they are privatized' (2019, 504). Our social existence increasingly unfolds within privately owned digital ecosystems where surveillance capitalists engineer and exploit behavioural patterns to maximise extraction. 'These private spaces are the media through which every form of social influence – social pressure, social comparison, modeling, subliminal priming – is summoned to tune, herd, and manipulate behavior in the name of surveillance revenues' (ibid., 504).

Consequently, what emerges is not an inclusive or participatory public sphere, but rather what Lippmann might recognise as a phantom public – a simulated space of engagement where the realities of behavioural manipulation and profit-driven governance supplant authentic collective discourse. This technological mediation doesn't merely modify publicness; it inverts it, demanding we fundamentally re-examine what constitutes a public when the very infrastructures of social interaction become instruments of private surveillance and control.

From proletarian to self-enclosed counterpublics

Among the many adjectival reconceptualisations of the public and the public sphere that aim to conceptualise epistemic enclaves – social groups or networks separated from alternative viewpoints or sources of knowledge, typically based on shared beliefs, identities and interests – as 'special' publics or public spheres, the concept of the *(proletarian) counterpublic* stands out for its originality and substantial departure from the normative and epistemic idealisation of the (bourgeois) public/ness. Taking Habermas' idea of the *bourgeois* public/ness seriously, Negt and Kluge critically conceptualised the *proletarian* public/ness as a historical counter-concept to that of bourgeois *Öffentlichkeit*, positioning it against hegemonic capitalist efforts to suppress, fragment or assimilate alternative forms of publicness directed at an autonomous organisation of the experiences and interests of the working class. The proletarian public, functioning as a negation of the bourgeois public, is a *preliminary* and *transient* form in which the interests of the working class develop. It is contingent upon three fundamental conditions: First, the interests of the productive class must serve as the driving force; second, a common medium that links the specific interests of the production sector and society at large must be established; and third, the inhibiting and destructive influences stemming from the disintegrating bourgeois public sphere must not exert overwhelming strength.

Tönnies had already articulated the need for the proletariat to struggle against the bourgeoisie for political rights and participation in the public

sphere. As the new bourgeois class rose in power, its ideas grew more prominent, successfully positioning its views as 'common property of the political
public'. Tönnies aptly outlined this dynamic:

> The entire struggle for freedom of thought, freedom of the press, and
> other civil liberties over the past few centuries is essentially an expres-
> sion of the struggle of the new bourgeois, national bourgeois class,
> which, as 'the society' – and often referred to as 'the people' or 'the
> nation' – campaigned for power, at first for participation in governance
> alongside the old estates and the monarchy that restricted their influ-
> ence, and increasingly, for exclusive rule. When this goal is achieved,
> the ruling class inevitably begins to hinder and restrict the class it rules
> in its possession and enjoyment of those liberties which it claims to be
> universal and necessary. The working class must then once again con-
> tend against it for the liberties it has promised for all but has secured
> only for itself. (Tönnies 1922, 128)

Negt and Kluge addressed the frustrating situation in which the proletariat had to fight for publicity against the bourgeoisie by posing two central
questions: 'What can workers do with publicness?' and 'What are the interests of the ruling classes with publicness?' (1972, 17). For them, it is crucial to
emphasise that the proletarian counterpublic/ness is not simply the opposite
of the classic bourgeois public/ness; rather, its essence lies in its emergence
from publics that are fundamentally shaped by capitalist interests. As they
argue, the organisation of social experience in the public sphere can either
serve the interests of a specific dominant (capitalist) class or promote human
emancipation (by the proletariat and its allies). From this perspective, the
concept of counterpublics illustrates the marginalised discussions that have
yet to break through into the general public sphere *by radically transforming it*.
If workers and the bourgeoisie are engaged in a discursive contest over 'what
constitutes the collective good rather than only fighting about it', this does not
yet signify a proletarian 'counterpublic' but rather 'an encompassing public
sphere, albeit an internally differentiated one' (Calhoun 2001, 1902).

The counter-public is conceived by Negt and Kluge (1972, 163) as a *preliminary* and *transitory stage in the formation of the proletarian public* (*Vorform von
proletarischer Öffentlichkeit*). While they also use the term 'counterpublic' in an
abbreviated form, this should not mislead us into overlooking its fundamental attributes – namely, its *class character* and (historical) *transitivity*. For Negt
and Kluge, the term 'proletarian counterpublic' does not simply denote the
opposite of the bourgeois public or represent a mere presentation of oppositional views, nor is it just a means of acting to implement the interests of a
specific social class. They are concerned with the diachronic sequential order

of forms, exploring the precursor/successor relationships between bourgeois and proletarian publics. Their conceptual framework envisions a potential societal transformation over time, aiming to foster the capacity to establish alliances among social forces that could bring about a comprehensive restructuring of society. The objective was not to pacify class contradictions but to drive revolutionary change rooted in the interests of the expropriated proletariat. Thus, a distinction must be made between social forces capable of carrying out a thorough societal reorganisation in the future and those (revolutionary) forces that are primarily focused on overthrowing outdated power structures under certain conditions (ibid., 167).

The term 'counterpublic' gained popularity following Negt and Kluge's work, notably within the English-speaking scholarly community.[1] Over time, it became widely entrenched in the examination of 'specific' counterpublics or counterpublic spheres, such as *subaltern, emancipatory, progressive, ideological, radical, feminist, republican, diasporic* and *post-colonial* ones. In recent studies, the counterpublic concept has undergone further adjectival proliferation with the exploration of *populist, Islamic, Islam-hostile, far-right, manosphere, anti-Euro* and *pro-AfD* 'counterpublics'. Unfortunately, the core features of Negt and Kluge's concept of the counterpublic – as a precursor to the transformative public – have been lost in translation and remain largely absent from the evolving discourse- and (id)entity-centred English counterpublic terminology.

The scholarly popularity of counterpublics, like publics, has further increased with the global internetisation of communication, which has brought with it various technological specifications for counterpublics, such as *online, networked, digital, Internet* or *platform* 'counterpublics'. It has also fostered studies on the *transnational* counterpublics emerging in 'a range of critical discourses globally', fuelled by the 'uneven distribution of resources and unequal access to power in the current phase of postcolonial late capitalism. [...] These counterpublics facilitate interests of disenfranchised groups to become visible and audible' (Dhawan 2012, 79).

In this evolving context, the concept of counterpublic is largely understood by analogy with antipolitics or 'negative' democracy, signifying opposition to or distrust in conventional politics and the rise of discourses of discontent. In contrast to Habermas' later claim that 'civil society has the opportunity

---

1 The term *Gegenöffentlichkeit* appears only seven times in the book (translated as 'counterpublic sphere'), while in the introduction to the English translation, Miriam Hansen (1993, xlvi) uses it 34 times, mostly as 'counterpublic'. However, she rightly emphasises that 'It is essential that the proletarian counterpublic sphere confronts these public spheres (i.e., *new public spheres of production*), which are permeated by the interests of capital, and does not merely see itself as the antithesis of the classical public sphere'.

of *mobilizing counterknowledge*' to acquire political supervision over 'the parliamentary complex (and the courts)' (Habermas 1992/1996, 372–373; emphasis added), the concept of 'counterknowledge' is 'expanded' in two directions. It aims to pinpoint the *collective bearer* of counterknowledge that emerges in response to the *hegemonic public*, characterised 'as spaces of withdrawal and regroupment', and 'as bases and training grounds for agitational activities directed towards wider publics' (Fraser 1990, 69). The generalisation of the public/counterpublic dichotomy beyond class differences supposedly implies alignment with a radical democratic ideal encompassing progressive movements and forces. However, it overlooks the class-based and transitory essence of the original concept of the *proletarian counterpublic*, as well as its critical epistemic value.[2]

In contrast, Negt and Kluge's concept of the (proletarian) counterpublic resonates powerfully through the idea of *contre-société* (counter-society) as 'nouvelle société' (new society), a notion articulated by Sue (2016) nearly 50 years later. A 'counter-society' challenges the existing system of 'the social contract' in which all 'modern values' – such as progress, work, integration or equality – have been definitively exhausted. Similar to Negt and Kluge's idea of the 'counterpublic' initiating a radical societal transformation, a new society is envisioned to emerge that will transform today's 'counter-society' into tomorrow's 'new society', based on digital social networks, the collaborative economy, shared knowledge and a commitment to the authentic meaning of political democracy.

Attempts to define the counterpublic as a universal concept, beyond Negt and Kluge's definition or Sue's understanding of counter-society, face serious epistemic challenges. The universalist (normative) public/counterpublic dichotomy assumes the universal existence of a hegemonic public (sphere) with an exclusive hierarchy or set of values and goals of the public agenda. This generalised synchronic notion of the 'counter-public' is inherently contradictory because publicness, by definition, normatively ensures the absence of exclusion. While this is an empirically unrealisable condition, it is precisely for this reason that the idea of publicness is considered a *counterfactual ideal* – a normative-theoretical idea(l) or 'golden standard' against which actual and

---

2 A clear example of this omission appears in a recent thematic issue of *Communication Theory* on 'Reconceptualizing public sphere(s) in the digital age'. While Negt and Kluge's work is briefly acknowledged in the editorial introduction (Eisenegger and Schäfer 2023), it is completely absent from the article that specifically addresses the topic of reconceptualising the counterpublic (Jackson and Kreiss 2023).

proposed (both theoretical and empirical) situations can be measured and evaluated.

Although assumed to be grounded in the principle of publicness, universally conceptualised counterpublics, like publics, actually operate outside of it, characterised by limited visibility and restricted access (Dahlberg 2018, 38). However, a fundamental contradiction arises when the counterpublic (sphere) is conceived as an *empirical* counterpart that challenges the hegemonic public (sphere) on the same normative basis of publicness, rather than through manipulative or instrumental counterpublicity – defined by Habermas (2022, 146) as 'a mode of semi-public, fragmented and self-enclosed communication [...] among exclusive users of social media that is distorting their perception of the political public sphere as such'. When publics and counterpublics coexist, intentionally or unintentionally conflicting or excluding one another due to limited accessibility, visibility or restricted communication codes, two possibilities emerge: (1) all may be considered counterpublics relative to one another or (2) at least some, if not all, may qualify as 'pseudo-publics' (Sorokin 1941/1992; Splichal 2012). Accordingly, a critical empirical analysis of the (counter)public sphere must focus on identifying and explaining these practical obstacles, with the aim of overcoming them and advancing towards the ideal of publicness.

The entitativity of counterpublics

In the current context, the term *counter*public is generally employed descriptively to refer to *social groups* and *categories* that 'articulate a counter status' (Asen 2000, 426), possess 'an awareness of [their] subordinate status', and perceive themselves to be in conflict with 'the dominant public' (Warner 2002, 86). This conflict arises not only from differences in ideas or topics under discussion but also from the specificity of discourse that 'in other contexts would be regarded with hostility or with a sense of indecorousness' (ibid).

Essentially, 'counterpublics' are understood as entities that see themselves, and are seen by others, as possessing inherent and enduring characteristics and identities essential to defining a genuine (entitative) social group.[3] Such 'counterpublics' may include ethnic minorities, diasporic communities,

---

3 In her book on feminist literature, Felski (1989, 168) refers interchangeably to 'the feminist counter-public sphere' and 'the feminist public sphere', attributing to them 'a dual function: *internally*, it generates a gender-specific identity grounded in a consciousness of community and solidarity among women; *externally*, it seeks to convince society as a whole of the validity of feminist claims, challenging existing structures of authority through political activity and theoretical critique'.

gender-based and other marginalised groups, as well as social movements (including conservative ones), online networks and other groups. Members of counterpublics are believed to share some common traits and a sense of shared fate, perceiving themselves as a distinct social group while defining their identity in opposition to the 'dominant public'. From their perspective, the dominant public may exhibit even more distinct (counter)group characteristics and vested interests. In summary, this conceptualisation of 'counterpublics' emphasises their *entitativity* or sense of 'groupiness' (Campbell 1958), as a defining feature – one that fundamentally contradicts the universal accessibility that is central to the principle of publicness.

The contradiction inherent in the conceptualisation of the 'counterpublic' lies in its dual nature. On the one hand, it is supposed to represent 'the public' itself (Warner 2002, 81); on the other, it contradicts the fundamental normative postulate that distinguishes the public from other social entities – its *lack of entitativity*. According to Park, publics are *transitional* and *temporary* phenomena, conceptually *opposed* to stable social groups, such as classes, sects or political parties. Publics lack a common past or future, self-consciousness and boundary maintenance. Members of a public typically do not share significant commonalities. Although they may temporarily share perceptions of empirical realities, they attribute different values to them, take opposing positions in debates and assert different interests (Park 1904/1972, 58). These internal oppositions and opinion clashes are constitutive of the public. Due to their diversity, individuals within a public neither identify as a unified entity – as 'we, the public' – nor seek to collectively determine their own actions. Consequently, both members and observers do not perceive the public as an enduring social group.

In contrast, if a collective – typically 'oppositional' – identity is identified as the defining feature of the '*counter*public', it becomes entirely separate from normative concepts of publicness and the public. In this sense, the counterpublic indeed functions as a kind of counterpoint to the ('dominant') public, or more simply, as a *non-public*. The key distinction between the public and the counterpublic obviously does not stem from the nature of their publicness but from entitativity. The absence of entitativity is a defining characteristic of the public, as entitativity strengthens with greater privacy within a group – the family epitomising the utmost privacy and the public representing its polar opposite. By emphasising entitativity as central to the counterpublic, this conceptualisation contradicts the inherent temporality of publics and blurs the distinction between (counter)publics and masses (and crowds), as well as between (counter)publics and social movements or non-governmental organisations. This effectively disqualifies the counterpublic as a genuine form of the public, shifting it away from the 'publicity end' towards the 'privacy end' on Bentham's 'privacy – publicity continuum', which is defined by 'the number of the persons to whom knowledge [...] is considered as communicated' (Bentham 1812/1827, 512).

In empirical terms, most entities commonly referred to as 'publics' – whether in the past or today – deviate from the normative conceptualisation of the public. This deviation reflects a broader trend of diminishing the public-worthiness of communication spreading particularly among social media users today. Like counterpublics, these exclusivist public–private entities are not based on the principle of publicness. On the contrary, they privatise publicness by instrumentalising the public sphere through promotional and disciplinary publicity, colonising it with private interests and topics and facilitating the institutional privatisation of communication. However, due to the absence of entitativity, no one recognises these (pseudo-)publics as counterpublics.

In the case of the proletarian counterpublic – conceived as an initial and transitory form of public emerging from a specific social category (the working class) – the term also implies a degree of entitativity. More importantly, however, it suggests the potential to transcend this entitativity through the historical process of abolishing class society and establishing a genuine public. These key aspects of the original conceptualisation of the proletarian counterpublic – rooted in the collective experience of proletarian marginalisation and expropriation, as well as revolutionary efforts to reorganise capitalist society – were often overlooked in later interpretations, especially with the extension of the counterpublic concept to right-wing populist movements with strong entitativity.

Such an extension of the concept exposes the problem of the *instrumentalisation of publicity*, which poses a serious threat to both publicness and democracy. In this context, mere access to information and the free dissemination of opinions can no longer normatively guarantee communicative rationality and freedom from hegemony. Indeed, the term *counterpublicity* may better capture this shift in the nature of communication – a shift characterised by irrationality, erosion of responsibility and an increasing blurring of the boundary between truth and falsehood, all exacerbated by the (mis)use of artificial intelligence.

There is no doubt that in an era of increasingly pluralised and diversified communication, the idea of a *unitary* public sphere has become untenable. Public sphere theory, primarily rooted in the values of Western civilisation, the Enlightenment and universalism, faces challenges concerning the conflictual nature of politics and the constitutive role of feelings and emotions in political identity formation. Yet, these challenges cannot justify the 'public–counterpublic' dichotomy. Instead, focusing on the influence of social structure, power dynamics and class interests on the formation of the public and public opinion in empirical research may provide a way forward, aligning with Negt and Kluge's emphasis on ruling class interests and possibilities for the underprivileged. This perspective opens up avenues to explore the possibilities and conditions to overcome the formation of opinion enclaves and foster an inclusive public sphere.

In contrast, the proliferation of adjectival modifiers – suggesting that virtually any form of communication can be seen as constituting some kind of public sphere, especially in empirical research – has turned the public sphere into a floating or empty signifier. By normalising counterpublics as a form of discursive self-organisation for underprivileged social groups, rather than addressing the conditions needed to eliminate their underprivileged status in the 'dominant public sphere', the conceptual diversification of the public sphere has blurred the distinction between the (counter)publics and *echo chambers.*

The concepts of counterpublic spheres and counterpublics inherently assume an *echo chamber effect*, where insular user groups are exposed primarily to, and actively seek, content that aligns with their own interests and ideologies. This dynamic exacerbates social divisions, fragmentation and political polarisation – directly undermining the normative ideals of publicness and the public sphere. Most online 'communities' today fail to transcend group particularisms, whether rooted in ethnic, racial, gender, age, ideological, religious, professional or other identity-based affiliations. The eclipse of consequential, authentic publics – if they ever fully existed – has accelerated as individual and corporate actors increasingly control access to online content. Consequently, monologues in fact-deprived digital rallies within fragmented pseudo-publics prevail over genuine, stimulating discussion and conversation in a true public. When communication occurs only among those who already share a specific opinion, ideology or status – where convincing arguments become unnecessary and barriers to dissenting views are reinforced – such interactions can hardly be regarded as expressions of the public. Rather, they resemble *pseudo-publics* or homogeneous *crowds.*

Technology-driven fragmentation of discursive interaction

Changes in the nature of the public and public opinion, along with the ways we understand and explain them, have always been closely linked to innovations in communication technology. Every technological breakthrough – from the seventeenth-century advent of the printing press, which mobilised and informed the public through printed materials, to radio, which Brecht envisioned as a participatory medium – has contributed to the

(re)conceptualisation of the public. Historically, public opinion was culti-
vated within physical spaces and print media, which early scholars regarded
as constitutive for the formation of the public. Today, however, digital platforms accessed through smartphones have become the primary spaces for
discourse. While the culture of reading books and newspapers was once considered essential to the Enlightenment public, the rise of digital communication culture and the decline in general education standards in some areas now
seem to indicate a decline in both reading culture and the idea of a cohesive
public.

The press played a pivotal role in constituting the public by providing a
platform for public expression and discussion that was previously inacces-
sible, facilitating the exchange of ideas crucial to democratic societies. Later,
radio and television commodified public communication, transforming it
into a mass-consumption format. While these media retained considerable
power to shape public opinion, their one-directional structure marked a
departure from participatory engagement. Bertolt Brecht, in his seminal critique of radio, lamented its failure to realise its dialogic potential, envisioning
a utopian model where listeners could become broadcasters – a prototype of
interactive media.

Despite their interactive potential to transform and activate the public
sphere, broadcasting technologies reinforced centralisation and passivity.
Unlike the dynamic exchange of ideas prompted by the print media of earlier
times or the collective deliberation in physical assemblies, broadcast media
produced a dispersed mass audience – individuals linked only by simultaneous consumption, not meaningful discourse. This shift epitomised what
David Riesman termed the 'lonely crowd': a society of atomised spectators.
Sociologists like Blumer and Mills further refined this analysis, distinguishing between inert 'masses' (shaped by top-down communication) and active
'publics' (defined by reciprocal debate), thereby recasting the classical crowd/
public dichotomy as a mass–public continuum.

Yet our full understanding of the technological substance of the public
only crystallised with the decline of print media, which had once served as
the self-evident foundation and 'organ' of the public – a substrate without
which, as Tarde argued, the public in the strict sense could not have been
constituted. As print media has waned, hybrid communication technologies,
such as digital platforms and social media, have redefined what constitutes a
public. In particular, the rise of AI has introduced new avenues for technological influence on publicness. Rather than merely channelling information,
these technologies now actively generate content and shape user engagement
in real time, exerting a powerful influence on how people perceive and interact with information.

The ascendancy of social media over traditional media marks a para-digmatic shift in how technological progress continually redefines both the nature of the public and the formation of public opinion. By placing interac-tivity and user-generated content at the core of public communication, these platforms have fundamentally restructured the infrastructure of publicness, enabling individuals to act as *prosumers* – simultaneously content consumers and creators. This evolution gave rise to what was once optimistically called the 'participatory' or 'networked public sphere', where opinion formation is continuous, decentralised and yet often fragmented. However, it has become increasingly evident that social media serve as far more efficient instruments of propaganda than the press or broadcast media ever were.

Historically, communication technologies have always inspired both hopes and fears – hailed for their power to connect and enlighten, yet feared for their potential to deceive, manipulate or control. They have been used and misused, cherished and cursed. Yet never before have these technolo-gies played as direct and active a role in shaping communication as they do today. Contemporary digital and AI technologies mark a profound shift, evolving from passive conduits into active participants in content creation and user engagement. No longer mere intermediaries, they now assume a quasi-governing role: disseminating norms, setting behavioural standards and structuring social interaction in ways that far surpass the influence of traditional media. Unlike earlier forms of mass communication, social media platforms and their algorithmic infrastructures actively shape not only what content circulates but also how opinions are formed, expressed and received. By amplifying certain voices and silencing others, these systems do not merely mediate public discourse – they engineer it. This transformation marks not just an evolution in communication but a revolution in the architecture of publicness itself.

In the digital age, which coincidentally began around the time Habermas' work on the public sphere was translated, technology's impact on shaping publics and public opinion has grown immensely powerful. The transition from analogue to digital, known as *digitisation*, has paved the way for *digi-talisation*: the transformative process of integrating digital technology across all sectors. A pivotal consequence of this transformation is *communification* – the pervasive integration of digital communication technology into virtually every facet of our lives. This shift compels all systems, including those that previously did not rely on communication technology, to operate through it. Enabled by Internet connectivity, globalisation and human-machine interac-tion, this integration has reshaped domains as diverse as economics, politics, science, education and culture. It has fundamentally altered how we commu-nicate, perceive and interact with the world, blurring the boundaries between work and leisure, public and private spheres and even bringing work into formerly work-free spaces, such as trains, cafés and our homes.

Communification has forged a direct link between communication and the realms of production and labour – a connection that was often disputed in the past but has now become too obvious to deny. Moreover, AI-driven communication algorithms and programmes now perform complex tasks once beyond human capacity – extracting, analysing and influencing opinions and behaviours through big data analytics – highlighting the unprecedented impact of communification.

This process has profoundly transformed and redefined the dynamics of public and private communication by seamlessly intertwining tangible and epistemic technologies, blurring distinctions between them. Tangible, or mechanical, technologies have traditionally constituted the material basis of wealth and power, shaping industries, economies and societal infrastructure – the foundational physical and organisational frameworks that enable societal functions. In contrast, epistemic technologies apply scientific knowledge to facilitate or transform knowledge production and comprehension, exerting a parallel but distinct influence as autonomous instruments of power. These epistemic technologies govern cognitive and informational dimensions of society: determining access to knowledge, establishing trust, shaping conceptions of truth and moulding norms and values.

By extending power beyond the physical into the realms of thought, culture and social organisation, epistemic technologies exert a profound influence that can either sustain existing structures or catalyse transformative change – depending on how they are developed, distributed and integrated within society. Their distinctive power lies in their capacity to operate at the foundational levels of cognition and social organisation without requiring direct coercion. By generating and disseminating information, knowledge and values, epistemic technologies shape individual cognitive capacities and social imaginaries; they influence norms and behavioural standards; and they regulate the interactions among individuals, groups and institutions.

The advent of digital communication technologies – especially the rise of social media – has radically altered the ways in which people communicate, interact and interpret the world. While these developments have enabled unprecedented forms of connectivity and participation, they have simultaneously introduced challenges that threaten the quality of discursive interaction – the processes of talking, discussing, debating and deliberating among citizens. At the heart of these challenges lies a technology-driven fragmentation of communication and thought, which disrupts collaborative meaning-making and hinders the formation of coherent public dialogue.

Initially celebrated as a catalyst for democracy and global integration, the Internet soon revealed its darker potentials. Beyond functioning as a platform for commercial profit, it evolved into a powerful surveillance infrastructure – monitoring user behaviour, profiling preferences and amplifying populist sentiment through algorithmic targeting. More troubling still is the emergence of the Darknet, accessible only via specialised software and often associated with illicit activities, opaque transactions and unregulated content. These developments complicate the ideal of an open, deliberative public sphere, revealing how technological mediation can simultaneously enable and subvert publicness.

Alongside the unintended social consequences that accompanied the evolution of new information and communication technologies, the Internet and smartphones have revealed intrinsic characteristics that, independent of user intentions, profoundly shape user behaviour. These technologies are not neutral tools; they embed design features that engage and manipulate attention, cognition and emotion. Neuroscientific research on human sensory and cognitive processing reveals a critical dimension of our digital engagement: although the human brain is exposed to approximately 11 million bits of information per second – comparable to the data required to stream a high-definition movie – our conscious mind is capable of processing only about 40 to 50 bits per second (DiSalvo 2017). This stark disparity reveals a persistent cognitive bottleneck, which becomes especially problematic in digital environments saturated with stimuli, where users are confronted with an overwhelming influx of information, including news articles, advertisements, status updates, algorithmically curated feeds and incessant notifications – all competing for limited cognitive resources.[4]

By their very design, social media platforms encourage multitasking, prompting users to rapidly switch between multiple conversation threads, notifications and stimuli that are rich in low-cognitive-intensity content and often elicit immediate responses. This architecture fosters an illusion of control, as users feel capable of absorbing and managing multiple streams of information simultaneously, while in reality sustaining fragmented attention. However, this notion of multitasking is deeply misleading. Not only is the

---

4 Research shows that the damaging consequences of the use of digital communication devices are especially threatening among young people. This is corroborated by PISA longitudinal studies of reading literacy, conducted in OECD member countries and economies since 2000, with around 700,000 15-year-olds tested every fourth year. The study reveals that reading literacy performance began to decline after 2012 and achieved an unprecedented 10-point drop – double the previous record – in 2022. This trend is particularly worrying as reading literacy is defined in a complex way to cover

human brain generally unequipped to handle multiple cognitive tasks simultaneously, but individuals also vary significantly in their capacities to interact with digital devices. As a result, cognitive energy is diverted into distracted presence and superficial engagement, diminishing the potential for deep understanding, reflexive thought and critical reasoning.

The implications of technology-driven fragmentation extend deep into how individuals process and interpret information. In the absence of physical cues – such as body language, gestures and vocal inflections – that are integral to face-to-face communication, the brain's natural tendency to assign nuanced meanings to behaviours and emotions is significantly impeded. In digital interactions, meaning must often be inferred solely from text-based exchanges, increasing the likelihood of miscommunication. Compounding this challenge is the prevalence of 'pop-up phenomena', in which sensational headlines or emotionally charged narratives dominate attention. This dynamic is further intensified by contemporary journalism's increasing reliance on clickbait strategies, which prioritise catchy, superficial content over depth and accuracy.

As the volume of information continues to grow exponentially, our capacity to engage with it meaningfully diminishes. Rather than facilitating deep engagement with complex issues, the prevailing communication culture encourages rapid consumption, where provocative headlines are too often mistaken for truth, and the subtleties of content are ignored. The fragmentation of discourse and the loss of contextual understanding create ideal conditions for the erosion of authenticity, allowing fake news, misinformation and conspiracy theories to proliferate. With each act of replication or reinterpretation, meaning drifts further from original intent, fostering a communicative environment prone to distortion, misunderstanding and manipulation.

This fragmentation is significantly amplified by the algorithmisation of social media platforms. Ironically, though these platforms were designed to empower users and foster authentic connection, they often undermine these very goals by exacerbating insecurity and inhibiting genuine engagement. Algorithms curate content based on past behaviours, preferences and interactions, leading users down a rabbit hole of increasingly homogeneous perspectives. As a result, exposure to diverse viewpoints becomes ever rarer, reinforcing cognitive biases and cultivating echo chambers. In such

---

students' capacity to understand, use, evaluate, reflect on and engage with texts to achieve their goals, develop their knowledge and potential and participate in society. Digital devices used for leisure, such as mobile phones – recognised as distractions by 30 per cent of students – seem to be associated with poorer results.

environments, users receive constant affirmation of their existing beliefs, narrowing the space for robust debate and critical reflection. The erosion of dialogical diversity undermines the very foundation of collective understanding, making it more difficult to engage meaningfully with complex societal issues.

This technologically induced fragmentation reshapes the conditions under which the public and public opinion are constituted and calls for a rethinking of their conceptual foundations. As individuals become increasingly insulated from dissenting views and primarily exposed to ideologically aligned content, publics are becoming more segmented and polarised. This results in the formation of discrete informational silos, where people with similar beliefs and social backgrounds cluster together, further entrenching their existing perspectives.

The consequences are both profound and systemic. The gradual erosion of shared interpretive frameworks significantly undermines society's capacity for cross-ideological understanding and civic empathy. More than merely deepening pre-existing social divisions, this dynamic actively corrodes the deliberative capacity essential to democratic governance. When citizens are no longer able – or willing – to engage across lines of difference, the foundations of publicness begin to erode. What is at stake, ultimately, is not just discursive pluralism, but the very bedrock of democratic society.

Chapter 2

PARADIGM SHIFTS

Habitual and Contractual Foundations of Publics

This chapter examines the transformation of the elitist conceptualisation of the (bourgeois) public by exploring how habitual behaviour and contractual arrangements influence public discourse, participation and opinion formation. While habits provide continuity and stability in public engagement, they can also entrench conventions that inhibit critical discourse. Conversely, contractual ties offer a formalised framework for interaction but introduce market logic that risks reducing public participation to transactional exchanges. The interplay of these forces not only redefines the ontology of publics but also reveals both constraints and opportunities for developing resilient forms of publicness in a digitised world.

The Corrupted Wealth of Publics

This introductory section revisits the Enlightenment's ideal of the public as a rational, critical agent underpinning democratic authority. Drawing on later empirical work in social psychology and sociology, it shows how group dynamics, cognitive biases and socio-economic inequalities undermine the utopian assumption of the public's high intellectual and moral integrity.

Habitual and Customary Roots of Public Opinion

Here the chapter explores how collective beliefs and public opinion are embedded in customary practices and everyday routines. It investigates how traditions, norms and everyday practices influence the ways individuals and groups form, share and reinforce opinions in the public sphere. Stressing the habitual and emotional nature of public engagement, it argues that deeply ingrained habits can both sustain a stable collective identity and stifle critical discourse. Particular attention is given to the ways digital technologies simultaneously reinforce old habits and disrupt them, creating novel modes of influence and interaction in the public domain.

Contractual Logics in the Evolution of Publics

The final section analyses the enabling and constraining role of contractual ties. highlighting their transformative potential in shaping interactions in public realms and fostering the development of publics. It traces the evolution of these ties from the newspaper era – when subscriptions and street sales shaped the relationship between newspapers and readers – to today's digital oligarchy, in which platform corporations deploy algorithmic systems to regulate user engagement and control content circulation. By illuminating how these contract-like mechanisms enable and constrain participation, the section underscores the need to rethink such dynamics in order to cultivate more inclusive, diverse and democratically vital publics.

***

In the liberal-democratic imaginary, the separation between the state, the market (capitalist economy) and the 'third element' that mediates between them – commonly referred to as civil society, where the public sphere and public opinion are rooted – occupies a central role. The autonomy of these elements is anchored in their distinct foundational and regulatory principles: the principle of free economic initiative and entrepreneurial freedom for the capitalist economy, the principle of sovereignty of the state and the principle of publicness for public opinion, among others. These principles not only underpin the unique functions of economic, political and societal domains, delineating the boundaries between them, but also structure the interactions and tensions among them. Together, they constitute the structural foundation of modern liberal democracy, enabling the coexistence of diverse yet interdependent spheres of authority and action.

Nevertheless, the practical interplay of these elements often reveals inherent contradictions, as their idealised autonomy frequently succumbs to (inter) dependence and contestation, challenging the very premises upon which this autonomy is based. Capital wields significant power over the state, influencing policy decisions and regulations through lobbying, financial incentives via 'public–private partnerships', information subsidies and contractual relationships. Conversely, the state seeks to regulate the economy with laws and policies intended to maintain order and protect the public interest. Yet, this regulatory power is often constrained by corporate interests that advocate reduced state oversight and prioritise market autonomy and corporate rights.

Moreover, powerful technology corporations often move forward at a pace that outstrips the state's ability to understand and/or respond effectively. Any attempts to intervene or impose constraints in turn frequently prove to be poorly conceived or ineffectual, showing the widening gap between the rapid evolution of technological innovation and the slow, reactive nature of regulatory frameworks. These dynamics illustrate the fragile equilibrium within liberal democracies, where competing forces are continually renegotiating the boundaries of influence and control, often to the detriment of both public accountability and the public good.

The weakest element in this dynamic is public opinion, caught between the competing demands of capital and political power. Media outlets, which should ideally serve as independent organs of the publics, increasingly operate under the converging influences of corporate consolidation, advertising imperatives and political interference through both propaganda and censorship. As a result, media actors often privilege these external forces over their fundamental democratic responsibilities: enabling transparent discourse and facilitating informed public deliberation. This subordination not only erodes the principle of publicness essential to democratic practice but also compromises their autonomy as impartial organs of the public.

The challenges to the autonomy of the public and the state, along with their independence from the economy, have intensified with the rise of surveillance capitalism. However, threats to media autonomy are not new; they have deep historical roots extending back to the absolutist state and the early industrialisation of the press. During this earlier period, media institutions faced political censorship and commercial pressures, establishing precedents for contemporary challenges to their independence. In today's digital environment dominated by corporate powers, these threats have only grown stronger. Media platforms are increasingly shaped by algorithmic logics that commodify information and user behaviour, reinforcing corporate dominance and constraining the capacity for independent, democratic discourse.

This evolution raises profound questions about the very constitution of the public – an issue that early thinkers grappled with when reflecting on the principle of publicness. Contemporary processes of communification and societal fragmentation under surveillance capitalism further complicate this challenge, undermining traditional mechanisms for the formation of the public and deepening divisions within and among various publics. These dynamics call into question the feasibility of maintaining a cohesive and inclusive public sphere in the digital age.

A genuine public cannot be established through discursive closure, the suspension of deliberative discourse or the formation of communication bubbles that circulate news and opinions exclusively within their own networks.

These traits resemble 'the suggestive influence exerted by people on each other', which – according to sociological classics – 'constitutes the deciding characteristic of the crowd [*Masse*]' (Park 1904, 23; 1904/1972, 19). Any entity claiming to be public avoids wholly abandoning *reflexive* publicity in favour of a purely instrumental form, such as the disciplinary and promotional publicity often associated with large crowds and masses.

Publics, of course, not only differ from other forms of mass behaviour but also – due to varying structural and historical-cultural conditions – exhibit unique characteristics that can vary significantly from one public to another. These differences appear even in essential aspects such as the ways and extent to which they assure the visibility and legitimacy of their concerns, as well as how deliberation is conducted. The real challenge of critical conceptualisation lies in bridging the gap between abstract principles and the concrete actions required to realise them. While defining *abstract principles* declaratively may not be overly challenging, the true test lies in translating these principles into *laws* and *contracts* that govern *practical action*. All genuine publics share an aspiration to embody the normative ideal of publicness to some degree, though this embodiment is inevitably shaped by prevailing social circumstances. Recognising these specificities is essential for understanding the complex dynamics of social and political engagement within any given context, which requires us to reflect on the concept's historical development.

To chart a way forward, it is therefore essential to step back and examine the historical lineage of publicness as a normative principle. Originally conceived as a universal principle, publicness sought to subject political power to rational scrutiny through publicity, closely linked to *personal freedom* – 'to the extent that it can exist together with the freedom of all others, according to Kant's famous formula' (Tönnies 1922, 258). Within this liberal framework, the feudal *representative public*ness that prevailed before the Enlightenment was seen as an aberration, a distortion of the very principle of publicness. This form of 'counter-publicness' was criticised for being manipulative and ceremonial, in stark contrast to the Enlightenment vision of a rational, inclusive public sphere.

Ironically, representative publicness – once the primary target of Enlightenment critiques – has re-emerged as the dominant empirical form of the universally conceived ideal of publicness. This resurgence is most evident in the proliferation of 'adjectival variants' of publics – formations defined by identity, affect or epistemic fragmentation – that are often uncritically designated as (counter-)publics or (counter-)public spheres, even as they prioritise particularistic interests over collective rational discourse. This paradox reveals a persistent tension between the normative ideal of publicness and its fragmented, often exclusionary, empirical instantiations. It underscores the urgency of revisiting foundational principles and devising operational mechanisms that can bridge this divide, enabling more inclusive, authentic and democratically grounded forms of public engagement.

The Corrupted Wealth of Publics

Enlightenment thinkers envisioned the public as the cornerstone of a system of authority grounded in open and rational discourse – an ambitious ideal that acknowledged the potential for collective enlightenment through free discussion. In this idealised model, individuals would engage in dialogue, form opinions and ultimately converge on a dominant perspective. Through the organised contestation of ideas, truth and justice were expected to emerge and guide societal action. Yet these thinkers were also acutely aware of the utopian nature of their vision. They recognised that publicity and open dialogue alone could neither prevent wrongdoing nor inspire virtue if the public chose to ignore critical issues. Nonetheless, they argued that without publicity, people would lack the means to challenge or inspire action on matters otherwise obscured from public view. The public was thus cast not as a passive audience but as an active discursive force – capable of challenging authority, holding power accountable and advancing collective moral and political development.

Publicity was considered essential not only as a channel for the exchange of ideas but also as a mechanism through which individuals could collectively scrutinise the actions and decisions of those in power. Yet the limitations of public participation soon became apparent, revealing the contentious assumptions embedded in the ideal of a rational public. While conceptually profound, this ideal has remained largely unrealised in practice. The exemplary bourgeois publics of the eighteenth and nineteenth centuries fell far short of the inclusive ideal they purported to embody. Vast segments of the population – most notably women, the less educated and the working poor – were systematically excluded from participation in public life. Moreover, as Mill observed,

> the public at large remain without information and without interest on all greater matters of practice; or, if they have any knowledge of them, it is but a dilettante knowledge, like that which people have of the mechanical arts who have never handled a tool. Nor is it only in their intelligence that they suffer. Their moral capacities are equally stunted. (Mill 1861/1991)

Such reflections highlight the persistent disjuncture between the normative aspirations of publicness and the structural and epistemic barriers that hinder its realisation. While the objective conditions for public discourse – such as the institutionalisation of publicity – were regarded as crucial, the central concern remained the intellectual and moral capacities of those who were expected to constitute the public. Without such capacities, the public could neither fulfil its deliberative function nor serve as a credible check on power.

As a subject of public reasoning and opinion formation, the public has never been understood as taking on a single or fixed shape. From its earliest conceptualisations, the normative-philosophical idea of 'the public' has implied a plurality of observable publics – comprising what Bentham (1781/2000, 163) referred to as 'an unassignable multitude of the individuals' – rather than a homogeneous whole. For Bentham, the public was a collective whose aggregated interests should inform moral and political decision-making. Yet, while the public appeared normatively unified – as the bearer of reason and legitimacy – Bentham empirically acknowledged its internal differentiation, suggesting the need to 'distinguish the public into three classes':

> The first is composed of the most numerous party, who occupy themselves very little with public affairs – who have not time to read, nor leisure for reasoning.
>
> The second is composed of those who form a kind of judgment, but it is borrowed – a judgment founded upon the assertions of others, the parties neither taking the pains necessary, nor being able, to form an opinion of their own.
>
> The third is composed of those who judge for themselves, according to the information, whether more or less exact, which they are able to procure. (Bentham 1791/1843, 582)

Further, Bentham observed that the second and third classes were often nested within 'particular communities' such as theologians, lawyers and merchants – each cultivating 'a public opinion of its own', shaped by *'esprit de corps*, corporate affections and specific interests' (Bentham 1843, 155). In contrast, 'the public at large' remained undifferentiated, chiefly due to a lack of specialised knowledge.

This tension between abstract unity and empirical plurality has remained central to subsequent debates about the constitution and role of publics in democratic governance. Echoing Bentham's differentiation, Kant also addressed the varying competences exercised by different publics – according to the general principle of publicness – in a process by which 'a public should enlighten itself' through the *public use of reason*. While Bentham's utilitarian conception of publicness focused on outcomes and collective welfare, Kant foregrounded individual rational autonomy based on intellectual self-determination.

Kant uses the term 'the public' to refer both to empirical and ideal groups, transcending particularistic interests in their public use of reason. Yet he neither explicitly defines these different publics nor systematically distinguishes between them. His primary concern lies in the individual's 'unrestricted freedom to make use of his own reason and to speak in his own person' from a universal and disinterested rather than personal standpoint (Kant 1784), in contrast to Bentham's focus on coordinated collective efforts to hold authority accountable through publicity. Rather than offering a fixed definition, Kant presents the concept of the public from multiple perspectives, integrating normative elements such as rational deliberation, political engagement, independent judgement and fidelity to universal principles of justice and human dignity.

Like Bentham, Kant conceptualises the public as hierarchically or thematically clustered. His ideal public assumes the role of a judge or scholar, 'who by his writings speaks to the public in the strict sense, that is, the world' (Kant 1784), and is uniquely qualified to form sound judgements, particularly in the formulation of laws and moral principles. Not everyone can contribute equally to every public; the value of one's contribution depends, among other factors, on their knowledge of the subject matter. This dynamic leads to the emergence of distinct 'issue publics' – each shaped by the legal and moral relations of its members to the issues at hand – or to an inwardly stratified general 'reading public'. Within this stratification, individuals are distinguished by their capacity for public reasoning, with the least involved, the 'outside, watching public' (*das äußere, zuschauende Publicum*), occupying the lowest tier.

Kant's differentiated understanding of the public is closely tied to his specific distinction between the *public and private uses of reason*, emphasising their different roles in societal and individual contexts. The *public use of reason* involves addressing others as members of a broader, unrestricted audience – often conceptualised as the 'reading public' – and is instrumental in fostering collective enlightenment. This concept reflects the exercise of reason in a free, critical and universal capacity, enabling individuals to transcend specific institutional roles or constraints.

In contrast, the *private use of reason* is bound by the specific obligations and responsibilities associated with an individual's role within an institution or profession. Here, reason operates within a framework of pre-established duties, contracts or organisational necessities, where unrestricted expression may be legitimately curtailed to ensure order, functionality or the fulfilment of a professional commitment. For instance, a military officer is required to prioritise discipline and adherence to orders over personal objections to commands to maintain operational coherence and authority among the ranks.

However, Kant insisted that even those operating within institutional contexts retain the right – indeed the duty – to participate in the public use of
reason outside of their professional roles. This nuance introduces a certain
ambiguity to his public/private distinction since individuals are simultaneously constrained by institutional obligations and empowered to critique
those very structures in their capacity as members of the public.

Kant attempts to resolve this ambiguity by distinguishing between the
general reading public, which he argues lacks the capacity to comprehend
complex scholarly debates and the scholars who constitute 'a different kind of
public – a learned community devoted to the sciences' (1798 /1979, 51), qualified to engage with and judge such works. He asserts that while individuals in
teaching roles (like clergy or educators) must adhere to state-sanctioned interpretations in their professional capacities, scholars must retain the freedom to
evaluate, critique and discuss ideas independently.

Scientific discourse within the academic domain lies, according to Kant,
beyond the sphere of the private use of reason and exceeds the comprehension of the general public. As it is highly complex and largely detached from
the concerns of everyday life, scientific debate is not suited for broad public
engagement. Nevertheless, scholars must retain the freedom to publicly evaluate and critique scientific ideas, guided by their expertise and conscience.
Moreover, since these debates are not directed at governmental authority but
are essential for the advancement of the sciences and humanities, the state has
no right to interfere in them.

In *Perpetual Peace* (1795/1939), Kant addresses the public from a legal and
political perspective, envisioning it as a collective body of citizens actively
engaged in shaping laws and governance. This political and legal role of the
public in a republican society is grounded in his principle of public law: 'All
maxims which stand in need of publicity in order not to fail their end, agree
with politics and right combined.' Kant argues that any political maxim that
depends on publicity to fulfil its purpose must align with the universal aim of
the public – namely, happiness – thus assigning politics the task of fostering
public satisfaction with their condition. Moreover, if political objectives can
only be attained through transparency – by eliminating public distrust in
political principles – then those principles must conform to the rights of the
public. Such alignment ensures the unification of individual and collective
goals within a framework of justice and mutual trust.

On the one hand, this legal perspective mandates that political decisions
and maxims conform to principles of justice and public trust, establishing a
necessary condition for the formation of the public. On the other hand, it
requires law-abiding behaviour from the public, underscoring their responsibility to uphold the legal framework that ensures its proper functioning. This

dual requirement creates a reciprocal relationship between political authorities and the public: political decisions must be transparent and just to earn public trust, while the public must demonstrate a commitment to the rule of law in order to sustain the legal and institutional structures of governance. This interplay is fundamental to the formation of a legitimate and functional public, where mutual accountability between governing institutions and public opinion ensures the stability and efficacy of democratic processes.

Nevertheless, in empirical terms, Kant's conceptualisation of the public use of reason – restricted to 'educated' or 'learned' publics – was culturally and sociologically constrained, as it excluded large segments of society. He effectively denied participation to all those who he did not consider 'self-dependent', referring to them as 'protected fellow subjects': women, workers, children and more broadly, anyone lacking property or the right to vote. While Kant thereby withheld from these groups the status of active citizenship and participation in legislation, he simultaneously emphasised the state's duty to enable individuals in a 'passive' condition to progress towards independence and an 'active' condition, ultimately acquiring full rights to freedom and equality. Like Tönnies and Dewey in later generations, Kant envisioned a future in which widespread education and rational communication would empower all individuals to develop the capacity for participation in the general public.

In today's context of intensified migration, globalisation and cultural diffusion, the legal aspect of the formation of publics outlined by Kant assumes heightened relevance, as it addresses the ever more complex dynamics of international and transnational relations. This perspective highlights the evolving distinctions between citizens and residents of a country concerning their relationship to – and potential influence on – state authorities through public opinion. Historically, theories of public opinion emphasised its capacity to transcend national boundaries, reflecting an era in which there was considerable overlap between citizen and resident populations (even though 'protected fellow subjects' remained excluded). This overlap reinforced the normative legitimacy and political efficacy of public opinion (Fraser 2007). In contrast, contemporary societies are witnessing a growing divergence between these categories, raising pressing questions about how non-citizen residents are included in public opinion formation and political deliberation; how rights and responsibilities are distributed; how identities are constructed in multicultural and post-national contexts; and how democratic legitimacy can be sustained when publics and public opinion reflect not only the perspectives of citizens but also those of an increasingly diverse resident population – and, at times, operate across transnational scales.

When the initial normative conceptualisations of the public were taken up by social psychology and sociology at the turn of the nineteenth and twentieth centuries, the utopian assumption of the public's high intellectual and moral integrity was challenged by empirical observations of group behaviour. These studies revealed that individuals' actions within public settings could be heavily influenced by social dynamics, pressures for conformity and collective decision-making processes, often diverging from the idealised standards of rationality and ethics. This shift gave rise to a more nuanced understanding of the public as a complex social formation shaped by the interplay of power dynamics, cultural norms and psychological influences.

Sociological perspectives have thus moved away from purely normative models, acknowledging the imperfections and vulnerabilities inherent in collective human behaviour as well as the existence of multiple publics to which individuals may simultaneously belong (Tarde 1901, 19). Park (1904/1972) introduced a key distinction between the crowd and the public, centred on how internal opposition shapes social dynamics. While the crowd suppresses differences among its members, responding uncritically and emotionally with a unified focus on a single object, the public, by contrast, emerges through the recognition of divergent values and interests. It is ideally characterised by rational discussion and deliberation, seeking consensus through engagement with difference rather than through enforced unanimity, thus enabling a plurality of perspectives among its members.

Among the many types of publics, the political public has always been considered the most significant. As Tarde observed, it was 'born, grew, and soon, in its overflow, absorbed all the other publics – literary, philosophical, and scientific – like a river absorbing its tributaries' (Tarde 1901, 12). From Tarde to Mills, sociologists have conceptualised the public as a multitude of 'scattered publics', recognising that 'the idea of the community of publics is not a description of fact, but an assertion of an ideal, an assertion of a legitimation masquerading – as legitimations are now apt to do – as fact' (Mills 1956/1999, 298). Whether Mills' analysis of the 'transformation of the American public into a mass society' (ibid., 297) captures an actual historical development or merely expresses disillusionment with lost democratic ideals is ultimately secondary to the evolving conceptualisation of the public itself.

The erosion of publicness in today's era of surveillance capitalism echoes the concerns raised by Mill and Tocqueville regarding the tyranny of the majority, which often manifests as intolerance towards minorities and disregard for dissenting views or (counter)arguments. In their attempts to safeguard the foundational principle of publicness from the perils of ill-informed mass opinion, both thinkers advocated for a prioritisation of *intellectual engagement* over *general accessibility* within the public sphere. This led them to the incorporation of elements reminiscent of representative publicness, akin to a feudal court, thereby facilitating what Habermas (1962/1989, 137) later described as the emergence of 'an esoteric public of representatives'. Through this controversial process of 'refeudalisation', the reflexive quality of publicity was preserved. Whether confronting the fragmentation of publics or the elitisation of public discourse, the resolution to what Dewey termed 'the problem of a democratically organised public' ultimately rests on the recognition that it is 'primarily and essentially an intellectual problem' (Dewey 1927, 126).

Contrary to the critiques of the nineteenth and twentieth centuries, which warned against the potential tyranny of the majority and underscored the importance of reflexivity in public discourse, current developments that reinforce elements of representative publicness now risk undermining reflexivity as a foundational quality of publicness. As the public sphere shifts from a space for critical discourse to a stage for manufactured visibility and performative display, it begins to resemble the instrumental and censorial logic of feudal publicity. While universal *access* to communication channels and the *visibility* of events deemed publicly significant remain essential for the public, the increased accessibility of communication networks and digital tools has enabled the amplification of visibility – even of fictitious events. Paradoxically, this democratisation of visibility has led to a decline in the quality of reasoned debate and contributed to the further fragmentation of public opinion.

The sheer volume and cacophony of voices in online discourse have eroded and marginalised publicness, despite the illusion of universal connectivity. Simultaneously, processes of communification have enabled manipulative practices, algorithmically filtered information flows and intrusive content curation, raising serious concerns about the authenticity of digitally mediated publicness. Although we are connected to a global network of information and people, this connectivity is often superficial, encouraging shallow interactions – such as button clicks and brief comments – rather than fostering sustained, meaningful engagement. The pursuit of virality has become a dominant force shaping online discourse, which is increasingly distorted by the pervasive presence of trolls and automated bots that manipulate narratives, disrupt dialogue and amplify provocative or polarising content to capture attention. Under these evolving historical conditions, the rational foundation of public discourse and the coherence of public opinion – both essential to democratic oversight – are steadily diverging from the Enlightenment ideals.

Habitual and Customary Roots of Public Opinion

With the rise of the public sphere as a conceptual framework, the behavioural dimension of the public – particularly its role in the generation and expression of public opinion – has often been marginalised. This shift towards abstract theorisation of the public sphere has sidelined the concrete, lived processes through which public opinion is formed, shaped and mobilised. Ongoing revisions of what constitutes the public and the public sphere point to an erosion of the defining features of normative conceptions of publicness and public opinion. In their place, we see the growing significance of complementary forms of social will, such as *habits, customs* and *contracts* – concepts elaborated by Tönnies and his intellectual predecessors. These behavioural and affective elements are increasingly central to understanding how publics are constituted and how publicness is enacted.

The task, then, is to reintegrate these behavioural dimensions of the public and public opinion into analyses of the public sphere. This reintegration underscores the complex layers of collective behaviour, including emotional, affective and psychological factors, as indispensable to understanding and cultivating the democratic potential of contemporary public engagement. Attending to these complexities and their interplay with habitual and contractual forms of social will-formation is essential for developing a holistic account of publicness. Such an approach must critically examine the conditions, possibilities and obstacles to achieving a deeper, more inclusive form of democratic interaction and collective will-formation – one that honours the rational ideals of Enlightenment thought while fully accounting for the embodied, affective, epistemic, economic, political and cultural complexities of social life.

One essential dimension of publicness is *habitual behaviour* – a concept introduced into modern philosophy by empiricists and utilitarians such as David Hume and John Stuart Mill. Although later taken up in psychology by William James, in pragmatist philosophy by John Dewey and in sociology by figures like Robert E. Park and Ferdinand Tönnies, habit has largely been neglected in recent theoretical debates on the public sphere. Yet, individual habits and their dependence on communal practices have become ever more relevant in attempts to explain online consumer behaviour and communication under surveillance capitalism, even if contemporary discussions rarely acknowledge the rigorous conceptual groundwork laid by earlier philosophers and sociologists. Revisiting the foundational work on habit and custom can thus enrich our analysis of how publics are constituted and function.

Habits and customs, often overlapping in their influence on behaviour, represent distinct forms of practice that operate at different levels of human experience. *Habits* are individual routines, typically formed through repetition, that, over time, become automatic or require minimal conscious effort. These routines often emerge as practical responses to everyday needs or situations, ranging from simple practices, such as reading the morning paper or watching the evening news, to more complex and often value-laden activities like embracing a vegan lifestyle or choosing public transport over private vehicles. Habits are shaped by individual preferences, contexts and environments, which makes them flexible and subject to change based on personal circumstances or deliberate intervention.

In contrast, *customs* are collective practices deeply embedded in the cultural, social or religious fabric of a community. They embody shared beliefs, values and norms, preserved through collective participation, often serving as a means of preserving identity and continuity across generations. Unlike mere repetitive behaviours, customs carry symbolic meaning and social significance, often formalised through rituals, ceremonies or traditions – such as weddings, national holidays, religious observances and the like. Habits and customs are deeply interconnected; because of their structured, communal nature, customs shape, reinforce and even instigate individual habits, transmitting them from one generation to the next.

From classical philosophical reflections to contemporary neuroscience of habit and purposeful behaviour, the study of habits and customs highlights their foundational role in human action and societal continuity, often revealing that entrenched habitual tendencies can outweigh momentary motivations. Early sociological thought likewise recognised the influence of habits and customs on public opinion, viewing them as indispensable to the formation of collective judgements and societal norms. However, later public sphere theories, with their dominant focus on rational-critical discourse and the institutional conditions for democratic deliberation, have tended to overlook these behavioural dynamics as the backbone of social interaction and public opinion formation. This omission is especially consequential in today's algorithmically mediated, integrated public-private digital communication networks, where individual habits are shaped by platform design and communal customs are reconfigured by globalised information flows, profoundly influencing patterns of participation and the contours of public opinion.

David Hume, for his part, regarded 'the principle of custom or habit' as 'the ultimate principle of human nature', without yet distinguishing between personal habits and collective customs. He argued that all inferences from experience depend on custom rather than on pure reasoning, making it 'the great guide of human life' (Hume 1748/2007, 32). Custom, he contended, alone renders our experiences useful by allowing us to expect future events to resemble those of the past: 'where it is strongest, it not only covers our natural ignorance but even conceals itself, and seems not to take place, merely because it is found in the highest degree' (ibid., 20). Absent custom or habit, Hume warned, 'we should be entirely ignorant of every matter of fact beyond what is immediately present to memory and the senses' (ibid., 33). For Hume, then, custom is the principle that lends coherence and predictability to human understanding and our engagement with the world.

Recognised for his assertion that it is 'on opinion only that government is founded' (Hume 1741/1777, 32), Hume highlighted the significant role of human opining in shaping society. He argued that 'opinion is a product of sympathy, which is more a result of mechanical influences from others than of pure reasoning' – essentially, a habit of the mind. According to Hume, our beliefs are shaped by habit and repetition: a 'contagion of ideas' that compels individuals to adopt views based on the emotional and intellectual impressions received from others, frequently conveyed through non-verbal cues and expressive communication. Despite this mechanical and habitual nature of opinion formation, Hume remained optimistic about the capacity for collective judgement to self-correct over time, trusting that 'the progress of learning and of liberty' could foster a community more resistant to 'idle rumor and popular clamour' (Hume 1748/2007, 539).

John Stuart Mill (1859/2001) offered a critical reassessment of Hume's claim that custom is 'the great guide of human life'. He argued instead that customs exemplify unreflective conformity to societal norms, warning that such conformity could pave the way to political despotism. Customs should not serve as a universal guide for human behaviour for a simple reason: They are typically designed for standard circumstances and temperaments, yet individuals often face unique situations or possess distinctive traits that these customs may fail to address. Even when customs are beneficial and suited to an individual, following them blindly can stifle the development of the unique qualities that define our humanity.

For Mill, genuine individual growth arises not from passive conformity to customary ways of behaviour but from reflexive, deliberate engagement. Essential human faculties – perception, judgement, discriminative feeling, mental activity and moral preference – are activated only through the exercise of *choice*. By adhering to customs without reflection, one forfeits the opportunity to cultivate discernment and to consciously pursue what is best. Mere imitation, whether in action or belief, fails to engage these critical cognitive faculties. If a person adopts an opinion without personal conviction or reason, their rational capacities may atrophy rather than flourish. Similarly, if one's actions are not guided by authentic feeling and character – aside from the obligations of affection or respect for others' rights – one risks rendering one's mental and moral capacities inert instead of nurturing a vibrant, active self.

Moreover, blind conformity to socially prescribed rules of thought and behaviour can have tyrannical consequences, stifling innovation and undermining a society's capacity for progress and self-improvement. Mill therefore, stressed the need to guard against 'the tyranny of prevailing opinion and feeling' and 'political despotism' by establishing clear limits on the legitimate influence of collective opinion over individual independence, thus balancing personal autonomy with 'the moral coercion of public opinion'.

Yet Mill's harsh critique of habit as merely an imitative exercise of human cognitive abilities lacked a substantive foundation. By contrast, Robert E. Park later observed that society and the established moral order are deeply rooted in tradition, custom and individual habits, making it impossible to dismantle them overnight by decree or legislation (Park 1904/1972, 93). Park understood custom as a communicative product bound up with reciprocal obligations – an essential feature of the constitution of a public. Only in a 'political society' – where the foundational social and economic order is upheld through competition and a public exists that encourages open discussion – do rational principles begin to supplant tradition and custom as the primary bases for organisation and social control, in contrast to societies organised around familial or authoritative structures. Even then, competition remains moderated by custom, convention and law; without these supports, law itself loses effectiveness. This complex interplay between the reflexive order of law and the spontaneous order of custom underscores the ongoing role of custom and habit in shaping social structures.

The paradoxical nature of habit is evident in Dewey's writing, where he observes that 'thinking itself becomes habitual along certain lines' and that 'habit does not preclude the use of thought, but it determines the channels within which it operates' (Dewey 1927/1946, 160). Dewey derived his understanding of habit from James, who argued that habit 'diminishes the conscious attention with which our acts are performed', simplifying the actions required to achieve a given result, increasing their accuracy and reducing fatigue (James 1890/2007, 114, 112).

Habits maintain societal order by keeping individuals within the constraints of their upbringing and roles, preventing social upheaval and stabilising professions, social strata and individual behaviours. They perpetuate divisions between social classes and 'doom' individuals to paths determined by early life choices, as changing direction becomes increasingly difficult with age – fostering stability but limiting adaptability (James 1890/2007, 121). This dual nature makes habit essential for social cohesion while simultaneously constraining personal freedom and mobility.

Drawing on James, Dewey highlighted the broader social assumptions and implications embedded in human habits, noting how these habitual patterns shape the pathways available to reflexive thought within society. Habits, on one hand, mirror and are shaped by social customs, while on the other, deeply rooted habits exert a powerful conservative influence, maintaining stability within society. Yet even though habits inherently lean towards conservation, they do not preclude change – instead, they guide its trajectory.

Among all habits, those of opinion prove particularly enduring. Dewey remarked that once such habits 'have become second nature, and are supposedly thrown out of the door, they creep in again as stealthily and surely as does first nature' (Dewey 1927/1946, 162). Over a century ago, he anticipated our contemporary concerns with misinformation and fake news by linking them to shifts in 'habits of opinion'. He argued that when these habits change, the initial effect is often disruptive – a disintegration of established beliefs – only to be replaced by 'floating, volatile, and accidentally snatched up opinions' (ibid.). Dewey further critiqued the media of his time, observing that while the volume of knowledge was increasing, it did not keep pace with the proliferation of fallacies and half-truths spread by careless newspaper reporting.

Dewey's insights into the resilience and vulnerability of 'habits of opinion' echo Tönnies' earlier analysis of how habitual and customary forces shape social will, laying the groundwork for a broader sociological inquiry into their influence on public opinion. In this tradition, Tönnies remains preeminent for the central role he attributed to custom and habit in the formation of social will alongside public opinion. He distinguished *habit* as an individual form of social will and *custom* as its communal or 'complex' equivalent – both foundational elements of *Gemeinschaft*. While in his typology of social will Tönnies argued that public opinion, as a specific and complex form of social will in *Gesellschaft*, 'cannot be equated with custom (*Herkommen*) or habit (*Gewohnheit*)', and should be differentiated from other forms of social will, such as 'an agreement that could change a legislature' or 'an established religion' (Tönnies 1916, 415), he also acknowledged that all these different forms of social will are interdependent in empirical reality

Well before writing his seminal *The Critique of Public Opinion*, Tönnies had explored these concepts in depth in his essay *Customs: An Essay on Social Codes*, published over a decade earlier. In this essay, he analysed the intricate and often contradictory relationship between habits, customs and public opinion – a relationship that remains as pertinent today as it was a century ago. While habit and custom were often used interchangeably before Tönnies, he drew a sharp distinction: habit pertains to individuals, whereas custom pertains to communities. Habit expresses individual *Wesenwille*, while custom represents an expression of social *Wesenwille*: 'Just as habit plays a decisive role in individual life, as man calls habit 'his nurse' and accuses it of being a tyrant, so we know that custom enjoys a superabundant power in the life of peoples and nations' (1909/1961, 42).

The core idea of his work on custom revolves around the observation that both individual habit and its communal counterpart – custom – hold a threefold meaning: (1) as a mere fact – an actual way of behaving; (2) as a norm – a general rule of conduct, where habit functions like a rule or a law; and

(3) as an expression of volition or will, which sets the norm. Tönnies considers this third aspect – the expression of volition or will immersed in thought and appearing as a free decision – as the least recognised yet most significant dimension (1909/1961, 29–30). This volitional dimension makes both habits and customs particularly relevant when examining another form of social will: public opinion.

The power of habits in human life stems largely from their alignment with the path of least resistance, as they render established routines the easiest course of action. Tönnies observes that 'established habits imperceptibly change into the instinctive. What we do habitually we do "unwillingly" just as we unwillingly make gestures, movements of welcome and of repulsion which have never been taught to us but in which we are skilled "by nature"' (Tönnies 1909/1961, 31). Unlike Mill, who strongly opposed individual submission to habits, Tönnies adopts a more balanced perspective, viewing both habit and custom as simultaneously enabling and constraining. They simplify life by automating behaviour, enabling individuals and societies to function with less effort and reflection. On the one hand, habits and customs prescribe specific actions and norms of conduct; on the other, they create space for greater freedom in discretionary activity.

Although opinions are frequently shaped and sustained by individual habits, and conditioned and prompted by customary thinking, they also hold the potential to transcend these habitual and customary influences, evolving into principles or convictions. When opinions reach this elevated state, they acquire a solidity capable of challenging and even dismantling the constraints imposed by habit. This newfound firmness resembles the steadfastness of faith: a trust or belief often associated with religious conviction, embodying a fundamental form of resolute will.

While habit and opinion generally coexist harmoniously, an inherent tension persists between them. According to Tönnies, this arises because thought, once it seeks independence, has a natural tendency to assert itself as the dominant force within the mind. As thought takes precedence, it motivates individuals to act with greater intentionality, transcending automatic, habitual responses. Reflexive thought, in this sense, cultivates distinctly human capacities by fostering growth through the conscious questioning and reshaping of one's beliefs. This reflexive process enables individuals to move from unexamined opinions to deliberate convictions, facilitating more engaged and self-aware participation in social life.

In contrast to Tarde (1901, 7), who regarded the *detachment from habits* as a defining feature of both the crowd and the public, Tönnies emphasised the intricate interplay between habits and public opinion. While conceptual abstractions, individual habits and social customs are integral to *Gemeinschaft*, they nonetheless manifest empirically in all forms of social organisation, including *Gesellschaft*. In theory, habit appears to contradict the rational principles upon which public opinion is formed. Yet in practice, the relationship between public opinion and habit represents a distinctive dynamic within the broader web of interrelated forces that bind *Gesellschaft* to its historical roots in *Gemeinschaft*.

Although public opinion can be conceptually disentangled from habitual and customary relationships in pure theory, the actual separation of normative categories of will is never fully realised in empirical life. Moreover, it is impossible for the entirety of rational self-consciousness to be separated from the spontaneous and instinctive dimensions of individual will. As such, complex forms of social will in *Gesellschaft*, such as public opinion, have foundational ties to *Gemeinschaft*, particularly in domains like religion (Tönnies 1887/2020, 243).

Tönnies' analysis highlights the profound influence of deeply embedded habits and the pervasive force of customs on the formation and expression of both individual and collective opinions. By (re)integrating these elements into public sphere theory, we can more effectively understand how habitual and customary behaviours shape, support or constrain democratic engagement and the development of public opinion. Traditions and institutions, shaped by centuries of trial and error, transmit not only stereotypes and prejudices but also a wealth of accumulated wisdom. Demanding that each generation rebuild everything from scratch would hinder our capacity to participate in a cumulative process of social learning.

Early sociological analyses revealed the pivotal role of habit in shaping human behaviour, notably in the formation of opinions. The complex processes through which individual and collective opinions emerge and are articulated cannot be overlooked in the study of publics and public opinion, where habits exert both enabling and constraining effects. Habits are not purely automatic responses; rather, they play a significant role in shaping subjectivity and influencing decision-making. Although habits can elicit instinctive and compulsive behaviours independent of rational thought – often functioning through subconscious mechanisms – they also shape future expectations, contribute to the formation of personal identity and mediate the interaction between human behaviour and technological environments (Kaluža 2022).

The persistence of reading habits and the habitual foundations of newspaper-reading publics, as noted by Tönnies, was vividly demonstrated in Berelson's 1949 study, 'What Missing the Newspaper Means.' In this study, Berelson observed that newspaper reading had become 'a ceremonial or ritualistic or near-compulsive act', and he underscored respondents' reflections on the habitual nature of their relationship with the newspaper:

> At least half the respondents referred to the habit nature of the newspaper: 'It's a habit [...] when you're used to something, you miss it [...] I had gotten used to read it at certain times [...] It's been a habit of mine for several years [...] You can't understand it not being there any more because you took it for granted [...] The habit's so strong [...] It's just a habit and it's hard to break it [...]'. (Berelson 1949, 126)

Similarly, during the era in which television emerged as the dominant medium, Lang (1962/2017) observed that the introduction of new communication technologies always produces habitual consequences. The arrival of television disrupted long-established routines, reshaping how people spent their disposable leisure time. Audiences for once-popular radio entertainment programmes declined sharply, movie attendance dropped and socialising outside the home experienced a notable reduction. Watching television became a routine activity, comparable to other habitual practices such as eating and sleeping, working and going to school, tending to the household, visiting the corner bar, shopping or reading the daily newspaper (Glick and Levy 1962/2017).

These sociological insights remain highly relevant today, as shifts in communication habits driven by digital and platform media continue to generate far-reaching effects that extend well beyond leisure and entertainment. We are currently witnessing a profound transformation in nearly all dimensions of public and private life, including how individuals access information, engage in discourse and form opinions. The rise of algorithmically curated platforms and personalised media environments has significantly altered the fabric of social interaction, often intentionally engineering user behaviour to foster compulsive habits. Moreover, these developments have reconfigured the public sphere itself, challenging the foundations of shared understanding, democratic participation and critical deliberation.

'Filter bubbles' and 'echo chambers', driven by recommendation systems based on algorithmic profiling, personalise the content presented to Internet users, often beyond their deliberate choices and without their conscious awareness. Recommendation algorithms curate distinct informational universes for individuals and groups, tailoring exposure based on habitual behaviour. The result is a diminished likelihood of shared experiences across a broader public, thereby fostering the emergence of epistemic enclaves. While these enclaves are commonly attributed to the design and operation of algorithmic recommendation systems, their formation is also conditioned by wider social factors and historical continuities. Fundamentally, such enclaves reflect the agendas of corporations, political actors and advertisers, whose interests are embedded into algorithmic architectures to maximise profit or secure influence by capturing and directing user attention.

However, the concept of the echo chamber alone does not account for the uneven distribution of informational access and the resulting isolation. It does not explain why certain individuals become immersed in such enclaves while others remain exposed to diverse viewpoints. On one level, human behaviour is shaped by normative expectations – what is perceived as the 'right' thing to do – driven by the desire for social approval, the influence of peers and the fear of exclusion. These dynamics foster conformity to dominant behaviours and opinions. Recommendation algorithms exploit this predisposition by amplifying content from 'friends' or familiar sources, much like early twentieth-century techniques of mass social engineering or the interpersonal manipulations of hacker social engineering in the 1970s, to make a product, service or activity appear more desirable and to increase engagement.

Yet, individuals' immersion in information enclaves may not solely result from algorithmic persuasion. Habitual content selection and routinised media consumption patterns also play a decisive role. These behaviours mirror long-standing tendencies, such as the habitual choice to read one newspaper over another, reflecting how custom and routine shape cognitive and affective orientations. The digital echo chamber, in this sense, is not entirely novel – it is a technologically intensified iteration of older patterns of habitual affiliation and epistemic closure.

The idea of publicness as a normative ideal stands in conceptual contrast to the entrenchment of everyday habits, customs and contractual norms. Yet in practice, instances of publicness are always materialised within concrete social frameworks – mediated by institutionalised norms, values and rules that simultaneously enable and constrain their enactment. These frameworks enclose publicness like a fence and impact its materialisation in practice. As Confucian thought reminds us, customs and traditions are not merely residues of the past but constitute vital resources for cultivating social harmony, ethical conduct and collective well-being – values that resonate with Enlightenment aspirations towards public reason and civic responsibility.

Nonetheless, this interplay between stabilising norms and the ideal of an open, dynamic and inclusive public sphere reveals a persistent tension. This is the tension between the continuity and cohesion afforded by customary practices and the critical, disruptive capacities of public reason and democratic innovation. Conceptually and empirically, this tension remains unresolved, not least because customs and habits have often been dismissed in modern public sphere theory as remnants of a bygone *Gemeinschaft*. However, the reintegration of habit into the theorisation of the public need not entail a wholesale redefinition of foundational categories. As Tönnies astutely argued, the basic constructs of social theory are not subject to empirical proof; they are normative propositions – recommendations grounded in logical reasoning rather than verifiable facts. Their value lies not in their demonstrability but in their capacity to guide critical reflection and ongoing theoretical refinement.

Contractual Logics in the Evolution of Publics

The evolving historical conditions brought about by digitisation and communification present new challenges to realising the principle of publicness. Historically, newspapers served as the cornerstone of the 'public opinion tribunal', providing the essential infrastructure for the formation, expression and influence of public opinion. They functioned as critical intermediaries, enabling the public to hold authority to account. In the early bourgeois era, newspapers uniquely contributed to cultivating what Gouldner (1976, 96) called 'enhanced public rationality', shaped by bourgeois profit motives and competitive enterprise. At the same time, newspapers became embedded in domestic routines, fostering reading habits that evolved into cherished customs passed down through generations. These reading habits profoundly influenced patterns of social interaction, public discourse and the institutionalisation of publicness. In societies with public broadcasting systems, early radio and television programming fulfilled a comparable role by shaping collective attention and discourse.

However, the formation of public opinion has historically depended not only on ingrained habits but also on contractual relations between newspapers and their reading publics. While habits governed interpersonal relations in informal contexts that required no explicit agreements, contractual frameworks became essential for structuring interactions that extended across more differentiated social realms – particularly those involving individuals from diverse backgrounds and unfamiliar contexts. Much like reading habits, informal reading contracts shaped communicative behaviour. Yet whereas habits functioned through tacit, organic processes, contracts formalised expectations and obligations, introducing elements of delineation and exclusivity. By establishing boundaries between reading publics and those outside them, these arrangements imposed structural closure on the public sphere – thereby complicating and, in significant ways, subverting the ideal of a universally accessible and inclusive public realm.

The contractual dimension of the public has been integral to its conceptualisation since the earliest theories of collective behaviour. Rousseau's notion of public opinion as the implicit will of collectives, for example, incorporates an essential contractual element, representing a distinct form of general will that differs both from the explicit will of assemblies and from the individual will oriented towards the common good. However, this contractual aspect of the public's behaviour should not be confused with the normative idea of the 'original contract' – a purely hypothetical agreement grounded in reason rather than empirical reality. Instead, it refers to practical contractual conventions, both explicit and implicit, that guide societal interactions. These conventions frame the ways in which individuals and groups engage with one another in the public sphere, setting boundaries for acceptable conduct and facilitating cooperative actions towards shared goals.

Contractual conventions refer to standard practices, customs or agreements that are widely recognised and followed in the formation, interpretation and enforcement of contracts. These conventions are not necessarily codified in law but are established through common usage and mutual understanding among parties involved. Unlike the abstract concept of the original social contract, these agreements are rooted in the social, political and economic realities of their time, reflecting the evolving needs and expectations of the public. As Durkheim wrote in *The Division of Labour in Society* (1893/1984, 158), a contractual relationship is never based solely on an agreement between parties involved; non-contractual elements are always present: 'Wherever a contract exists, it is submitted to a regulatory force that is imposed by society and not by individuals': Any agreement rests on an invisible array of institutions, state law, social customs and shared habits, generating the underlying consensus and trust without which contracts would be impossible.

More than a century ago, Tarde and Tönnies were among the first to recognise the emergence of commercial-contractual relations within public opinion. Tönnies (1922, 35) criticised the conditions under which 'selling the expression of an opinion and using it for one's own benefit is an act of personal freedom', thereby transforming opinion directly into 'an object of exchange, a thing for sale' – in other words, into an impersonal commodity. In a similar vein, Tarde (1901, 16) described the commercialised public as a 'very deviant species of commercial clientele' that establishes a social bond between 'people of the same world' based on shared consumption patterns – from the products they buy to the newspapers they read. Tarde's critical portrayal of the public as 'amiable look-alikes who seek to reinforce their similarity and differentiate themselves from what they are not' closely resembles what we today call an *echo chamber.*

Lippmann, while not postulating a direct contractual bond between newspapers and the reading public – one that would render the reader liable for breach of loyalty or the publisher accountable for misinformation

– nonetheless envisioned the potential utility of 'competent tribunals, prefer-
ably not official ones, where charges of untruthfulness and unfairness in the
general news could be sifted' (Lippmann 1922/1991, 330). The very notion of
a 'competent tribunal' implies an implicit contractual bond between media
institutions and the public, one that warrants oversight and may be enforced
through reputational or normative sanctions.

As Tönnies observed, in *Gesellschaft*, the contract replaced the role that custom played in *Gemeinschaft*, for 'contract is the custom and creed of commerce'
(Tönnies 1887/2020, 258). Unlike the familistic newspaper reading habits
conceptually rooted in kinship-based community life, the commercial relationships between newspapers and the public reflect the complex dynamics of
a contractual society. Newspapers, as central organs in the formation of public
opinion, were simultaneously corporate actors embedded within the capitalist
economy – structured by private ownership, advertising revenue and market
competition. The contractual relationship between newspaper proprietors,
advertisers and readers was thus fraught with structural contradictions – contradictions famously discussed by Marx that rendered the press vulnerable to
subordinating its public-service role to commercial imperatives. This tension
threatened to undermine journalistic ideals of accessibility, transparency and
civic accountability, as market logic increasingly superseded ethical standards
and the normative principle of publicness. These contractual arrangements,
by departing from ideals of public accessibility and transparency, risked sur-
rendering newspapers entirely to the hegemonic forces of the capitalist market rather than upholding ethical commitments to the principle of publicness.

Whereas the influence of habit on the constitution of publics and public
opinion has demonstrated remarkable historical continuity, the dynamics of
contractual relations between media institutions and publics have undergone
profound transformation in the current era of communification. The contractual nature of public opinion is now shaped by platform owners who determine the terms of access and participation in digital environments. Unlike
traditional print media, constrained by physical distribution and subscription
models, online content is accessible to anyone with an Internet connection.
However, this accessibility comes with an intensification of contract-based
regulation – governing the interactions among platform providers, advertisers and users. In this context, user participation and autonomy within online
communication networks are often curtailed by corporate control over content and data flows (van Dijck 2009). Engagement with digital platforms
requires users to enter into what can be described as a *pact with the digital devil*,
exchanging access for the commodification of personal data, exposure to
algorithmic surveillance and acquiescence to opaque and unilateral terms of
service. These arrangements highlight the increasingly asymmetrical nature

of digital contractuality, wherein users are compelled to conform to the platform's conditions – conditions that are rarely negotiable and overwhelmingly reinforce the power of corporate actors at the expense of public agency.

Driven by the imperatives of the surveillance economy and accelerated by advances in artificial intelligence, a digital oligarchy is emerging in which a small number of transnational corporations wield disproportionate power. This concentration of influence bears a striking resemblance to the economic and political dominance once exercised by feudal lordships. In this new regime, vast segments of the Internet's infrastructure are being privatised, allowing these corporate entities to exert de facto control over the legislative, executive and judicial dimensions of Internet governance – now effectively components of proprietary rights embedded in platform ownership.

This power is not confined to the digital domain; it spills over into offline life, shaping user behaviour, social norms and even democratic governance. As Burtell and Woodside (2023) warn, these developments are transforming 'our information environment so significantly so as to contribute to a loss of human control of our own future'. While states have made efforts to regulate the digital realm – primarily to safeguard data privacy and mitigate harmful or illegal content – these initiatives seldom challenge the foundational issue of corporate ownership and control. Even when legal frameworks are introduced, their efficacy is often constrained by enforcement limitations, jurisdictional fragmentation and the agility of corporate actors to adapt or evade. The rapid deployment of AI technologies further exacerbates these dynamics, intensifying the refeudalisation and oligarchisation of the public sphere. As concerns mount over the far-reaching consequences of unregulated AI, leading experts have urged that '[m]itigating the risk of extinction from AI should be a global priority, alongside other societal-scale risks such as pandemics and nuclear war' (CAIS 2023).

A defining feature of the Internet's oligarchic transformation and the resurgence of feudal-like control over public discourse is the hidden influence exerted by corporations through artificial intelligence and recommendation algorithms. This dynamic gives rise to a *personalisation paradox*: de-humanised and de-personalised recommendation algorithms personalise mass-generated content to make it more attractive for individual users. Yet, in the absence of regulation, these algorithms operate opaquely, subtly nudging users towards particular behaviours – such as joining like-minded groups, reinforcing pre-existing opinions or making targeted purchases – often without users' awareness or informed consent to the algorithms' potential effects on their choices and behaviour.

Like opinion polls, recommendation algorithms influence – and potentially erode – the conditions for political subjectivation and collective action. Just as those who finance polls exercise de facto control over how public issues are defined, algorithmic curation exerts substantial influence over users' perceptions, often prioritising narratives aligned with the interests of the platform owners or content sponsors. In this way, algorithms function as instruments of control, distorting the contours of authentic public discourse and narrowing the range of viewpoints by constructing a skewed representation of 'public issues'. Both mechanisms – polls and algorithms – undermine autonomy, inhibit critical reflection and reduce human agency, echoing Tönnies' century-old critique that the press increasingly served the interests of political parties rather than operating as a genuine organ of the public.

However, important differences remain. Whereas 'polls elicit, organize, and publicize opinion without requiring any action on the part of the opinion-holder', thereby transforming public opinion 'from a behavioural to an attitudinal phenomenon' (Ginsberg 1989, 278–279), algorithms encourage and shape user engagement by tailoring content to individual preferences and behavioural profiles. This interactivity can foster a sense of participation, but it also risks confining users within epistemic enclaves that limit exposure to dissenting or unfamiliar perspectives. Unlike polling, which passively captures and reflects existing opinions without demanding action, algorithms actively curate, amplify and reinforce specific content based on data collected from user interactions – thus entrenching belief systems and deepening polarisation. While they simulate participatory involvement, recommendation algorithms simultaneously undermine the deliberative quality of public discourse and challenge the foundations of democratic engagement.

The emergence of new forms of public expression has made it more difficult for authorities to navigate public opinion than during the era dominated by polling. Traditional opinion polls tend to dilute the influence of individuals with strong convictions by aggregating them into a broader, often more apathetic, 'mass public'. For governments aiming to appear responsive, it was more convenient to align with the numerical preferences reflected in polls than to contend with more disruptive or direct expressions of sentiment – such as petitions, protests, strikes or open letters. In this context, polls functioned as a form of 'collective statement of permission' (Ginsberg 1989, 276), allowing policymakers to frame their actions as publicly endorsed. By contrast, the fragmented, volatile and often polarised outputs generated by powerful recommender systems complicate such alignment, increasing political vulnerability and making public opinion less predictable and less governable.

This unpredictability is exacerbated by the limited control users have over the algorithmic curation of information. The content users encounter is increasingly shaped by opaque systems that shape both content and user beliefs, limiting access to diverse news sources and narrowing the range of available opinions. The dominance of a few AI-driven tech giants – entrenched through contractual arrangements and enabled by regulatory inertia – grants these corporations unprecedented influence over not only online interactions but also the broader social and political environment. Their concentrated control undermines the principle of universal access to information and constrains the conditions necessary for inclusive public discourse. In such an environment, opinion enclaves proliferate, intensifying polarisation and undermining the integrative function of the public sphere. Consequently, the formations that emerge under these conditions – shaped more by algorithmic sorting than deliberative engagement – often fall short of meeting the normative criteria for even preliminary manifestations of genuine publics.

Historically, contractual relationships were typically restrictive and narrowly defined, regulating specific exchanges or obligations between contracting parties, while at the same time forming part of an objective totality of communicative relations that structured public life. This framework allowed individuals who coalesced as 'a public' through their contractual engagement with newspapers to remain strangers, independent from one another – failing to recognise themselves as participants in a distinct collective entity, even while being objectively connected to all through this shared contractual relationship. By preserving the impression of impersonal deliberation and collective reflexivity, this abstraction of the contractual connection among its members made it possible for the public to emerge.

In the era of communification and AI, Internet users may still remain strangers to each other and maintain anonymity in peer interactions. However, they are anything but anonymous in relation to corporate platform owners and their business partners, who accumulate vast amounts of user data through opaque surveillance and extractive infrastructures.[1]

In this context, contractual arrangements have shifted from reciprocal obligations between parties to one-sided, utilitarian transactions imposed by platform providers. These arrangements are typically structured around convenience, efficiency and individual gratification, with little regard for the social bonds or collective concerns that normatively underpin the formation

---

1 A recent report by the Irish Council for Civil Liberties found that the online activities and locations of individuals in the European Union are recorded on average more than 300 times a day. Real-Time Bidding (RTB) data reveals highly sensitive information about a person, including their location and movements over time, what they read, watch or listen to, sexual interests and personal problems. RTB data is used not only to track the movements and online activities of individuals but also to sell intimate information about targeted individuals and their organisations to corporate or political clients seeking to influence, blackmail or hack them (Ryan and Christl 2023).

of publics. Users are encouraged to act as atomised individuals, guided by algorithmic cues and behavioural nudges, rather than as participants in a shared communicative space. This utilitarian model of contractuality undermines the foundational conditions necessary for the formation of publics: mutual recognition, shared concern for the common good and reflexive engagement. As such, publics cannot be meaningfully realised within the framework of platform-driven digital contractuality, which privileges data extraction over democratic interaction and perpetuates asymmetrical power relations between users and corporate actors.

If the relations between users and media platforms were governed exclusively by contracts, this would inevitably foster a hierarchical communication dynamic in which corporate owners and platform managers retain structural power, while users are positioned as passive subjects lacking agency to influence the terms or architecture of engagement. Such arrangements stand in stark contradiction to the democratic ethos of the public sphere. Yet, the opposite extreme – complete deregulation – is not a viable option either. In the absence of structured governance, the public sphere risks being dominated by entrenched habits, customs, traditions or prevailing market forces that suppress critical discourse and democratic pluralism. Unregulated communicative environments can also reinforce social exclusion, marginalising individuals and groups unfamiliar with – or noncompliant with – dominant cultural norms.

This structural tension is especially evident in the surveillance economy, where corporate platforms have radically reconfigured their relationships with users. As Zuboff (2019, 88) argues, a critical turning point occurred when Google reversed its founding stance against advertising in favour of corporate growth and profit maximisation. The shift from serving users based on their search intent to targeting them through behavioural data marked a suspension of earlier principles of user trust and transparency. This 'exceptional' logic – which prioritises commercial surveillance over reciprocal obligation – exemplifies how the commodification of user data distorts the conditions of public interaction and undermines democratic engagement. What emerges is a profound tension: on the one side, contract-based governance – driven by profit and market imperatives – reinforces inequality and erodes public agency; on the other, the absence of regulatory structuring risks entrenching exclusion and weakening the deliberative potential of the public sphere. Navigating this tension is essential for reimagining a public sphere that fosters democratic life rather than subverts it.

* * *

The convergence of habitual, contractual and digital transformations marks a paradigmatic shift that redefines the contours of contemporary public life. Normatively conceptualised publicness – once anchored in deliberation – has given way to performative visibility, orchestrated by algorithmic metrics. Stable newspaper publics have dissolved into transient, transactional interactions, structured by opaque digital infrastructures. This erosion of clear boundaries between public and private realms, intensified by surveillance capitalism, reconfigures both the means and meanings of participation, paving the way for the emergence of the *gig public* – a fragmented, platform-mediated form of discursive engagement.

Habitual behaviours provide a sense of continuity, yet risk entrenching norms that inhibit critical discourse. Contractual arrangements, while offering structure, often commodify public interaction, especially within digital contexts. The rise of digital platforms under surveillance capitalism has further exacerbated these dynamics, consolidating power in a digital oligarchy where algorithmic governance and data extraction distort authentic public discourse and fragment collective opinion.

Together, these shifts destabilise the conditions for social cohesion and democratic continuity, calling for new frameworks to understand agency, normativity and relationality in a world shaped by rapid and often disorienting transformation. Acknowledging the entanglement of these modes of regulation is essential for theorising a renewed social architecture capable of sustaining democratic life amid evolving uncertainties.

Chapter 3

THE GIG PUBLIC

Redrawing the Boundaries between Public and Private Realms

This chapter examines the transformative impact of surveillance capitalism on the evolving relationship between public and private realms in the digital age. It examines how the structure and logic of Internet-mediated communication have redefined these boundaries, reshaping not only how visibility, participation and engagement are configured but also how power, agency and identity are distributed. Particular attention is given to the evolving contractual relationships between platform owners, content creators, service providers and users, which are increasingly governed by asymmetrical terms and algorithmic infrastructures.

The Will to Visibility: From Representative to Performative Publicness

This section explores the shift from traditional, representative forms of publicness – where individuals participate as observers in public representation of power – towards performative publicness, characterised by self-presentation and visibility-driven engagement. Social media platforms encourage both individuals and institutions to prioritise spectacle and self-promotion over substantive interaction, fostering a regime in which actions or utterances are 'performed into existence' or 'brought into being' through public display. This shift fundamentally alters the nature of public participation and discourse, privileging presence over deliberation.

From Print to Platform: The Evolution of Publics

This section focuses on the emergence of gig publics – temporarily assembled constellations of audiences and content creators convened via digital platforms. The nature of the public has undergone a dramatic transformation, shifting from the stable, cohesive structures of the newspaper era to the fragmented, ephemeral forms of the digital age. Whereas newspaper publics were anchored in shared experiences, institutional authority and sustained engagement, gig publics are fragmented, ephemeral and mediated by algorithms, operating within the constraints of surveillance capitalism.

'Hop-on-Hop-off' Discursive Sightseeing: Roaming the Landscapes of Publicness

This section critiques the transient and superficial nature of contemporary computer-mediated discourse. Users increasingly participate in fragmented discussions, skimming across issues without sustained attention or deep engagement. The 'hop-on-hop-off' model likens this behaviour to a tourist's superficial engagement with destinations, where users momentarily join discussions before swiftly moving on, thereby undermining the potential for meaningful deliberation and long-term commitment to public concerns.

The Structural Immaturity of the Gig Public: The Habitual, Contractual and Algorithmic Enclosure of Reason

This section investigates how, within the AI-driven evolution of communication, the gig public becomes entrapped in a self-perpetuating system where habits, contracts and algorithms foster intellectual passivity and contribute to democratic decline. Algorithmic mediation often infantilises users by reducing their autonomy and agency, locking them into habitual patterns of engagement dictated by opaque AI logic. This 'yoke of immaturity' reflects a broader stunting of critical faculties, as AI systems prioritise efficiency, convenience and behavioural control over reflexive engagement.

* * *

The dominance of the surveillance economy on the Internet – particularly through the AI-driven commodification of both user attention and intention – has profoundly transformed the relationships among the key 'contracting parties' in the digital world: platform owners, content and service providers and users.

In this book, I deliberately prioritise the term *surveillance economy* over more commonly used descriptors such as *attention economy*, *gig economy* and *platform economy*. While all four terms capture critical aspects of the contemporary socio-economic order – and often coexist – they emphasise distinct dynamics.

The *attention economy* focuses on the commodification of human attention; the *gig economy* highlights the precarious, fragmented and task-based nature of digitally mediated labour; and the *platform economy* refers to the technological infrastructures and intermediaries that organise work, sociality and consumption. Yet none of these terms fully encapsulates the contractual architecture of visibility, data extraction and behavioural governance that increasingly defines public engagement in digital environments.

By contrast, *surveillance capitalism* (Zuboff 2019) more clearly exposes the asymmetrical contractual relationships that underpin participation in mediated public spaces. Whether through consent to opaque terms of service, algorithmically nudged self-performances or involvement in datafied publics, individuals are drawn into tacit or explicit contractual arrangements that shape not only their visibility but also their roles as producers of value and meaning within the public sphere.

In the context of the *gig public*, this contractual logic becomes central. The public, within this paradigm, is no longer conceived as a deliberative assembly or a spontaneous social formation, but as a configurable discursive grouping, temporarily assembled through algorithmic cues and behavioural incentives and continuously monitored and moderated in real time. These publics are not primarily shaped by social or political norms, but by the operational logic of surveillance capitalism, where *visibility* functions simultaneously as the condition and the currency of participation. The surveillance economy foregrounds how visibility has become a governable and extractable resource – captured, quantified and repurposed within a system of predictive behavioural control. It offers the most compelling analytical framework for understanding how both publicness and privacy have been reshaped and how the dynamics of public discourse have been redefined under conditions of commodified user engagement and algorithmic surveillance.

In capitalist mass society, the once-idealised 'marketplace of ideas' – a space for open, reasoned deliberation among informed citizens – has undergone a profound metamorphosis. Rather than operating as a democratic forum for the exchange of diverse perspectives, the public sphere has become a contested terrain dominated by media manipulators, platform owners and algorithmic curators competing for control over attention and opinion. In this reengineered environment, the public largely assumes a passive and reactive role: individuals receive and respond to strategically crafted content designed to shape perceptions, emotions and behaviours. This shift corrodes the deliberative and participatory ideals historically associated with the public sphere, replacing them with asymmetrical power relations that consolidate influence in the hands of the digital corporations that control both the infrastructure and the narratives of public discourse.

Normatively, the public sphere has been imagined as an open and all-accessible realm of deliberation, where strangers convene to discuss issues of social consequence, free from their particularistic interests. In contrast, the private sphere has traditionally represented a more exclusive and personal domain, characterised by habitual, intimate interactions among a smaller circle of closely associated individuals. These realms were once conceptualised as mutually exclusive, each governed by its own norms and rules.

However, the advent of integrated public–private digital communication networks and platforms, alongside hybrid modes of interaction, has fundamentally altered the conditions in which publicness and privateness are generated, maintained and potentially compromised. *Integrated public–private communication networks* refer to digital infrastructures – primarily social media platforms and messaging services – where public and private modes of communication coexist seamlessly within a single technological platform *for the first time in history.* These networks enable users to shift fluidly between traditionally separated modes of communication (one-to-one, one-to-many, many-to-one, many-to-many) and types of content (text, image, audio, video and voice) on a global scale, often with nothing more than a change in privacy settings, audience selectors or interface context.

This integration blurs long-standing boundaries between public and private spheres, creating dynamic and overlapping communicative spaces in which a single post or interaction can serve multiple social functions simultaneously or sequentially. Private interactions may unexpectedly gain public visibility, while public discourse may take on the intimacy and selectivity characteristic of private communication.

These networks are particularly significant for enabling contextual fluidity: Users do not merely alternate between public and private modes but often participate in hybrid interactions that defy simple classification. Integrated public–private communication networks, therefore, do not just support both types of communication – they entangle them, reshaping how publics are formed, how intimacy is performed and how social visibility is negotiated across increasingly porous boundaries.

This transformation, propelled by advancements in communication technology, has deeply affected the evolution of both publicness and privateness. The heightened permeability of the boundary between public and private domains has facilitated unprecedented levels of visibility. For individuals and organisations using digital tools for personal branding, public campaigns or advocacy, the likelihood of gaining public attention has markedly increased.

However, this expanded visibility comes at a significant cost to personal privacy, which -- unlike the privileged privacy of corporations – is often poorly protected. The concept of 'privacity' (Splichal 2018) captures the growing imperative to assert and protect privacy in an environment increasingly dominated by digital publication. It refers to the measures individuals and organisations must take to protect personal and corporate privacy in an environment where privacy is often compromised for the sake of publicity and visibility.

This dynamic reveals a troubling asymmetry: While corporations benefit from stringent data protection regimes that secure intellectual property and proprietary information, individuals remain vulnerable to relentless data harvesting and behavioural tracking. Their personal information is continuously extracted, repackaged and monetised for corporate gain. Even as users adopt 'digital hygiene' practices – such as managing privacy settings, employing encryption or limiting data disclosures – these efforts often fall short in mitigating the risks of exploitation within a system structured around the will to visibility, where publicity is privileged over privacy, and both are commodified.

The Will to Visibility: From Representative to Performative Publicness

The will to visibility – a dynamic, and potentially irrational force that compels individuals and groups to seek attention, gain recognition and participate in shared social spaces – represents a double-edged sword in democratic life. Like the will to power, it is rooted in the human need for self-affirmation and meaning-making. People want their existence and actions to matter, and being visible in society is a way to affirm that.

Alongside universal access, visibility is essential to preventing marginalisation and social exclusion. When visibility is restricted, certain groups may be excluded, leading to epistemic enclaves and elitism. Conversely, when the will to visibility is unbounded –unmoored from reason or shared standards of discourse – it can distort deliberative processes, fragmenting the public into spectacle-driven interactions, superficial engagements and populist performances.

The central challenge, then, lies in reconciling the will to visibility with the norms of rational-critical debate: striking a balance between enabling expressive freedom and ensuring that public discourse remains reflexive, inclusive and constructive. This tension sits at the heart of modern democracy – and arguably constitutes one of the most urgent theoretical and practical challenges in efforts to revitalise publicness today.

In pre-Enlightenment societies, the will to visibility was channelled through symbolic and ceremonial acts of power, governed by institutional hierarchies and cultural codes. Visibility was a privilege reserved for elites,

expressed through *representative publicness* – a mode in which authority figures staged displays of power or virtue before passive crowds. Habermas
(1962/1991) describes representative publicness as a premodern form of public life in which authorities (e.g., sovereigns, clergy and nobility) 'represented'
their power and status through theatrical gestures, rituals and spectacles, not
through dialogue or deliberation.

In the era of mass media, traditional outlets such as print newspapers,
radio and television maintained near-monopolistic control over visibility for
more than a century. Through curated interviews, editorials, feuilletons and
talk shows, these media institutions determined who could appear in public,
how they were framed and under what conditions. Yet editorial principles
and criteria were often shaped by commercial imperatives or political affiliations – positioning editorial offices in traditional media as instruments of both
creating and censoring visibility.

The digital age has profoundly altered this architecture. The will to visibility has become at once more individualised and more systemically mediated.
On the one hand, platforms have democratised access to visibility, enabling
individuals to broadcast themselves without the mediation of traditional editorial hierarchies. On the other, that visibility is now governed by platform-
specific norms, algorithmic sorting and behavioural incentives structured by
surveillance capitalism. Visibility is no longer simply a matter of personal
expression; it is entangled with platform design, commercial interests and
algorithmic optimisation.

Thus, the will to visibility today is both an internalised drive for recognition
and a structural condition governed by systems of data extraction and value
generation. It manifests in everyday habits – likes, shares, posts and reactions
– but is also shaped by contractual obligations and algorithmic infrastructures that determine who is seen, by whom and for how long. Within this
framework, the will to visibility becomes a key mechanism through which
attention is commodified and publicness is reconfigured.

Rather than being a pure and autonomous expression of self-affirmation,
visibility has become a commodified resource – produced, distributed and
governed by hidden forces such as data-driven algorithms, behavioural analytics and corporate interests. In this reconfigured system, the pursuit of visibility is no longer merely an act of personal empowerment but is embedded
within a system of exchange where visibility is mediated and often commodified. Individuals contribute content, perform presence and generate engagement, but these acts of expression feed into a system designed to extract data,
predict behaviour and monetise participation.

The more individuals seek visibility, the more they become enmeshed in
a self-reinforcing feedback loop: heightened participation begets algorithmic

reward, which incentivises further performance and engagement, deepening individual dependence on platform logics. In this way, the communicative pursuit of recognition becomes structurally analogous to gig labour – precarious, contingent and governed by invisible market forces. Just as gig workers operate under algorithmic control and opaque ratings systems, users striving for visibility navigate a constantly shifting terrain of algorithmic affordances that they neither control nor fully comprehend.

This dynamic underpins the commodification of visibility, where acts of public expression are no longer valued primarily for their content or contribution to democratic discourse but for their capacity to generate engagement metrics and advertising revenue. As visibility becomes a traded commodity, publicness is increasingly shaped not by deliberative ideals, but by the imperatives of platform capitalism.

Since the Enlightenment era, the creation of visibility through publicity has been associated with transparency, democratic openness and the resistance to censorship. However, publicity can also function as a form of coercion. *Imposed* visibility – where individuals or groups are made public without consent or adequate protection – can constitute a form of surveillance-based tyranny, eroding the protective boundaries of privacy and exposing individuals to reputational harm, data exploitation or targeted manipulation.

This tension points to a crucial normative distinction between different forms of publicity. *Critical publicity* is reflexive and dialogic: It seeks to foster public awareness, stimulate reasoned discussion and draw attention to issues of enduring collective concern. It aligns with the democratic ideal of publicness by promoting participation, accountability and the contestation of dominant narratives.

By contrast, *instrumental publicity* refers to communication driven by strategic or operational objectives, often disconnected from the ideals of deliberation or collective reasoning. Its primary aim is to instrumentalise visibility for particularistic ends. Instrumental publicity may serve *promotional* purposes (e.g., influencer marketing, brand visibility) or *disciplinary* functions (e.g., algorithmic surveillance, behavioural nudging).

In its disciplinary form, instrumental publicity renders individuals visible in order to normalise, monitor or constrain behaviour – transforming visibility into a mechanism of social control and suppressing diversity. It ultimately restricts individual autonomy and threatens both privacy and publicness by transforming the invisible into the visible – or vice versa.

Meanwhile, *promotional publicity* – typically employed in corporate advertising, propaganda and public relations – creates a representational spectacle focused on curating appearances. It promotes what users ought to think and believe exists, rather than critically reflecting on or accurately representing what actually exists.

Ultimately, the commodification of visibility and the proliferation of instrumental publicity reveal its ambivalent character. While visibility can empower and include, it can also exploit and dominate. Any meaningful defence of democratic publicness today must reckon with this ambivalence – seeking to disentangle visibility from its commodified and disciplinary forms and to re-anchor it in practices of critical, participatory engagement.

Yet even beyond the realm of promotional and disciplinary logics, visibility continues to exert a powerful influence on personal identity and self-perception. In the contemporary media landscape, the desire for visibility manifests not only through strategic or externally imposed forms but also through self-directed performances of publicness. Whereas promotional and disciplinary publicity are typically aimed at shaping external perceptions or behaviour, *performative publicity* originates from within the individual, oriented towards self-expression and the cultivation of personal visibility.

Performative publicity refers to communicative acts that are intentionally staged – designed to create an impression or convey a particular identity or behaviour to an audience. It centres on the individual's or group's action of presenting themselves in a public space, often in pursuit of social recognition, validation or identity construction.

Performative publicity thus functions as an agent of self-representation, driven by the *will to visibility*, which has become a central force in contemporary media culture, where individuals actively strive to have their presence perceived and acknowledged. In digitally mediated environments, where the boundaries between publicness and privacy are becoming increasingly porous, the will to visibility is entangled in two parallel and contradictory processes: the *privatisation of publicness* and the *publicisation of privacy*. These dynamics are transforming interactions between individuals and platforms, with profound implications for citizens' rights and freedoms.

As publicness is amplified by people's growing access to online expression, the value and distinctiveness of publicity appear to diminish, while 'the more the value of privacy increases, the more it is pervaded by publicness' (Trenz 2024, 93). Privacy is either voluntarily alienated or involuntarily appropriated, further undermining traditional distinctions between private and public life. In this process, both privacy and publicness are commodified, public discourse is co-opted for corporate gain and the foundations of authentic public engagement are eroded. It also becomes evident how deeply the social significance of the *publicisation* of privacy is tied to the human *will to visibility* – a drive akin to the will to power – culminating in the emergence of *performative publicness*.

The *privatisation of publicness* in the digital age mirrors the commercialisation of physical public spaces, such as parks being repurposed as venues for private events. 'Public spaces' that historically facilitated public discourse – whether in privately owned clubs, pubs or through newspapers – have now been supplanted by platform-mediated environments governed by corporate profit motives. Political and cultural debates, as well as community-building activities, are increasingly mediated by private corporations whose overriding goal is to monetise users' attention and visibility. Integrated public–private communication networks, originally designed to enable collective discourse, are now largely controlled by digital corporations like Facebook, X (formerly Twitter) and YouTube. While these platforms serve as arenas for 'public' interaction, their private ownership allows participation and access to be regulated based on corporate interests – often prioritising commercial objectives over democratic engagement through content moderation, recommendation algorithms and access restrictions.[1]

Seemingly free access to these networks conceals a deeper process of commodification. Platforms, supposedly designed to enhance user experience, monetise user data to convert attention and behaviour into tradeable commodities for targeted advertising and behavioural manipulation. Surveillance technologies employed by platform corporations enable them to shape user norms and regulate activities in ways that align with corporate interests. These dynamic transforms publicness into a commodity governed under corporate control.

Platforms segment users into algorithmically curated discourse enclaves. Features such as paywalls on news websites, subscription-only content and premium platform tiers contribute to a system of unequal information access. In this stratified system, wealthier users enjoy access to premium content and deeper insights, while less affluent users are relegated to ad-supported, often lower-quality content, perpetuating informational inequalities. These dynamics underpin two prominent forms of epistemic enclaves: filter bubbles and echo chambers. A filter bubble arises as a side effect of personalised recommendation algorithms, which filter out or exclude certain relevant

---

1 In a recent controversy, Meta, the parent company of Facebook and Instagram, has faced mounting criticism following reports of censorship – including blurred or blocked posts, downranked or blocked searches and deleted accounts – targeting a range of 'potentially sensitive' words and Democratic- and Palestine-related content. At the same time, the company has loosened its content moderation rules, ended corporate diversity programs and discontinued third-party fact-checking. See: https://www.forbes.com/sites/esatdedezade/2025/01/21/meta-faces-backlash-as-democrat-related-terms-disappear-from-instagram.

voices or perspectives from the recommended content. In contrast, an echo chamber represents a more deliberate result of actively discrediting or excluding alternative or dissenting voices. By perpetuating cycles of misinformation and narrowing the scope of critical engagement. Platforms reinforce epistemic segregation – the fragmentation of information ecosystems into isolated enclaves.

Yet these mechanisms of epistemic segregation not only fragment public discourse but also reflect a broader trend: the commodification of both information and personal data. As platforms curate content to maximise user engagement, they simultaneously blur the boundaries between public and private spheres. This convergence facilitates the *deprivatisation of privacy* alongside the privatisation of publicness. Although these processes move in opposite directions, they yield similar consequences – diminishing individual autonomy and subjecting both public expression and private information to corporate control. The deprivatisation of privacy manifests in two distinct forms: *voluntary publicisation*, where users willingly share personal information online and contractual *corporate appropriation*, where individuals 'agree' to terms in often opaque, heavily one-sided agreements that grant corporations extensive control over their data.

Corporate appropriation of privacy involves the extraction, datafication, exposure and commodification of individuals' personal lives, locations, preferences and behaviours by external entities, notably digital platforms and corporations. Amplified by digital and AI technologies, this process reshapes (notions of) privacy, with considerable implications for individual autonomy, societal norms and the broader concepts of privateness and publicness.

While the consequences of the deprivatisation of privacy resemble those of the *commercial appropriation of identity* – a subset of the broader offence of the illegal invasion of privacy – the deprivatisation of privacy itself represents a more systemic and pervasive phenomenon. It encompasses the collection, aggregation and commodification of big data, frequently affecting entire populations. Unlike the unauthorised and illegal commercial use or theft of an individual's identity or data, deprivatisation operates at the structural level of contemporary surveillance capitalism. It entails the continuous transformation of personal data into a currency used to trade future attention and behaviour as commodities in exchange for access to the creation and consumption of online content. This process is facilitated by technological infrastructures and corporate practices that blur the boundary between consent and coercion.

For attention to become commodified, it first needs to be habitualised. As William James (1890, 286, 552) observed, our empirical thoughts are shaped by 'habits of attention', which determine what we register as experience. Habitual repetition enhances the retrieval or remembering of information from memory, yet something may appear repeatedly without being registered as experience unless we direct our focus towards it. Conversely, even a single meaningful encounter, if noticed deliberately, can leave an enduring impression. This dynamic of habits of attention highlights the power of digital platforms in shaping what individuals habitually notice, which in turn triggers habitual behaviour. As behaviour becomes habitual, actions are initiated more impulsively than through conscious motivation, and when habitual behaviour is spontaneously activated, alternative behavioural responses become less cognitively accessible. As a result, while influencing public discourse and the formation and expression of public opinion, this spontaneous activation of communicative actions can lead to a public that is *reactive* rather than *reflexive* – a phenomenon that can be termed the *gig public*.

In contrast to the corporate appropriation of privacy, the *publicisation of privacy* involves individuals voluntarily transforming personal experiences, behaviours, identities and other aspects of their private lives into publicly accessible content – typically through digital platforms and social media – in order to gain visibility, social capital or financial rewards. This shift fosters a performative construction of the self – a persona created by individuals who curate and present their lives to align with societal or platform-specific norms and meet audience expectations, thereby prioritising visibility and the corresponding public approval they seek over authenticity. By prioritising the creation and consumption of emotionally engaging, often personal content, social media algorithms encourage users to share personal, even sensitive, aspects of their lives, as such content tends to attract more attention. Individuals, especially young users, often feel compelled to participate in this system to achieve visibility and recognition, even when they might otherwise prefer to keep certain aspects of their lives private.

Platforms like Facebook, Instagram, TikTok and X have habitualised the *publicisation of privacy* in order to re-privatise it. They incentivise users to commodify their lives, turning private, sometimes sensitive experiences and events into branded content or entertainment to stimulate user engagement and attract sponsorships. This engagement transforms their private data into measurable metrics such as likes, shares and comments, which the platforms use to optimise algorithms, refine content targeting and increase advertising revenue. In this way, privacy, through performative visibility, becomes the most profitable commodity. As personal moments are repurposed for public consumption and corporate gain, turning private life into a public spectacle, the line between private and public becomes ever more blurred.

Corporations like Google and Meta further contribute to the deprivatisation of privacy by collecting vast amounts of personal data through online tracking, user interaction analysis and integration with third-party data sources. Internet users are often required to link their online activities to identifiable profiles, further diminishing the space for privacy by making personal information accessible – not only to the platform but also to advertisers, third-party entities and even other users. Moreover, the content and data we generate and share often concern others, rendering us vulnerable not just through our own disclosures, but through the actions of others who may be overly generous or careless with their data. The growing capabilities of big data analytics and AI to aggregate and analyse vast datasets – uncovering behavioural patterns and insights that transcend individual datasets – further amplify these vulnerabilities.

In the integrated public–private digital networks controlled by platform corporations, individual data protection is fundamentally inadequate. As individuals, we cannot fully comprehend the implications of the information we disclose once it is aggregated with millions of other data records. Consequently, individual concern for data protection is insufficient; effective privacy protection requires collective coordination. The interconnected nature of digital data makes privacy a public good – its benefits are shared collectively. Therefore, safeguarding privacy requires shared responsibility and coordinated efforts among individuals, communities and institutions at the international level.

The publicisation of privacy gives rise to *performative publicness* – a reimagined form of the pre-Enlightenment mode of *representative publicness*, which was rooted in the elitisation and instrumentalisation of visibility. Historically associated with courts and the nobility, representative publicness emerged as a form of elite visibility rooted in the display and performance of status. Its instrumental nature was notably praised by Machiavelli (1513/2006), who advised that a prince should always '*show*' in his actions greatness, courage, gravity, and fortitude' and '*show* himself a patron of ability', while also 'entertain[ing] the people with *festivals and spectacles*'. As he emphasised, 'He must *present himself* as an example of courtesy and liberality, while always maintaining the majesty of his rank' (emphasis added). This pre-Enlightenment form of publicness centred on theatrical authority and symbolic containment.

While representative publicness originated as a mode of elite theatricality, centred on symbolic authority and social hierarchy, its evolution under liberal modernity retained many of its exclusionary traits. Despite its rhetorical alignment with universalist ideals, the bourgeois public sphere often functioned as a curated space of visibility – preserving symbolic control while selectively amplifying voices deemed legitimate. This tension between democratic inclusion and representational containment persisted across identity-based publics and counterpublics, which, although expanding the boundaries of participation, frequently reproduced epistemic enclosures and visibility hierarchies.

In contemporary, communified societies, the publicisation of privacy has contributed to a further transformation: the rise of *performative publicness* – a digitally mediated mode of visibility centred not on elite display but on doing, acting and creating for public attention. Unlike its representative predecessor, performative publicness is not grounded in institutional authority but in personal exposure, aesthetic expression and algorithmic amplification. Both representative and performative forms of publicness are mediated by socio-technical infrastructures that manage visibility and engagement, yet they are governed by different logics: Representative publicness seeks legibility for power, whereas performative publicness seeks attention for presence. Understanding their contrasting dynamics – as well as the hybrid formations that emerge between them – is essential for rethinking how publicness might be renewed in an era of algorithmic mediation.

In the contemporary context, these two modalities of publicness diverge across multiple dimensions. Representative publicness, instrumental to the *will to power*, stabilises and channels discourse by compressing collective energies – attention, demands, outrage – into legible formats through selective representation. Rallies, processions, parades and media campaigns exemplify such forms, designed to interface with power structures like the legal system, political bodies or the press. Rooted in symbolic authority and delegated voice, representative publicness reduces complexity through abstraction, filtering participation via customs, norms and institutional procedures. Its core function is to transmute individual or collective expression into procedurally valid inputs – policy proposals, courtroom arguments, parliamentary motions – that feed the bureaucratic machinery of prevailing power structures.

Performative publicness, by contrast, is propelled by the *will to visibility* and self-presentation. It manifests through algorithmically curated affective expression – posting, sharing, commenting or protesting online – and thrives on immediate user engagement. Rather than relying on institutional filters, it is governed by personalised algorithms, habitual interaction patterns and platform-governed norms that regulate attention and visibility. While this mode enables broader expressive participation, it is prone to volatility in the absence of stabilising mechanisms, evident in phenomena such as virality, flame wars and user burnout. Yet these chaotic dynamics may serve a stabilising function of their own – not through consensus-building but by diffusing public attention in ways that prevent structural disruption.

These forms are not mutually exclusive; they frequently coexist within digital platforms, where the tension between symbolic containment and affective overflow is continuously negotiated. Representative mechanisms strive for coherence through institutional rituals – appointing spokespersons, producing reports or initiating lawsuits – translating dispersed engagement into recognisable, actionable forms. Performative excess, however, resists such containment, generating waves of visibility that can overwhelm, subvert or redirect institutional attention. This tension reveals the structural instability of platform-driven publicness: an oscillation between personal expression and institutional representation, between deliberative coherence and viral intensity.

This oscillation can be further illuminated through Hannah Arendt's conception of publicness, which centres not on rational discourse, as in Enlightenment thought, but on appearance. For Arendt, the public realm (*der öffentliche Raum*) is a 'space of appearance' in which individuals reveal themselves through action: It 'comes into being wherever men are together in the manner of speech and action and therefore predates and precedes all formal constitution of the public realm and the various forms of government'. Publicness, in this view, is achieved not through deliberative reason or formal political participation, but through visibility – through actions that are witnessed, acknowledged and shared within a collective space. In this framework, self-presentation becomes central: Individuals attain recognition and affirm their unique identity through their capacity to appear before others (Arendt 1958, 198).

In the context of platform capitalism, Arendt's emphasis on appearance underscores the performative dimension of digital publicness. To appear, to be seen and to be registered – algorithmically, affectively and socially – becomes a mode of political being, even when it escapes or evades formal representation. Visibility itself becomes a form of power: the power to shape one's narrative, to influence public perception and to mobilise collective attention.

Access to this public realm has historically been limited to those whose identities or actions were deemed worthy of display. The space of appearance was largely reserved for those who required 'the presence of others before whom they can appear' to present their 'work' – such as performing artists and politicians – as well as for 'those things whose essence it is to appear and to be beautiful' (Arendt 1961, 218). Like Hegel, Arendt believed that courage is required to leave the safety of private life and step into the public space, where exposure carries both the risk of vulnerability and the possibility of recognition. This belief brings her understanding of public space close to the 'will-to-power'; by living together, people not only generate the public realm but also create the power that sustains it.

Yet Arendt also cautions that this will to power can stem from a sense of frustration or impotence – a drive to overcome one's limitations and assert control over oneself or the world. Precisely because of this origin, the will to power can easily metastasise into domination or tyranny. In this light, even the ostensibly open architectures of digital platforms do not escape these dynamics. The pursuit of visibility – amplified by algorithmic incentives and attention economies – may reproduce older hierarchies of attention, reinforcing cycles of exclusion, distortion and spectacle. What appears as democratic openness often masks a deeply stratified terrain, where the space of appearance remains unevenly distributed, and performative publicness becomes a volatile, precarious form of political being.

Following the reasoning of Machiavelli and Arendt, we might conceive of the *will to visibility* as a defining force of contemporary public engagement. It reflects the conditions of modernity, where the individual is both empowered and compelled to act in a world in which self-representation and visibility play significant roles in shaping social and political dynamics. Whether through activism, personal branding or cultural expression, the desire to be seen recalls Machiavelli's advice to captivate the public imagination and Arendt's insight that people create power by appearing before one another. *The will to visibility, then, is not merely a desire for recognition – it is a political drive to assert presence and claim space within a shared and contested world.*

The collective participation and consciousness from which power in the public realm arises are precisely what the will to visibility seeks to exploit in order to shape narratives, influence perceptions and leave a lasting mark on public discourse. As both Arendt and Machiavelli have suggested, this tendency is a double-edged sword: While the pursuit of visibility and dominance in the public realm can empower individuals, it can also foster manipulation, oppression and ultimately undermine democratic principles. This enduring tension challenges Enlightenment ideas of publicness and sets the stage for the emergence of the gig public.

The concept of the will to visibility is crucial when examining how the desire for visibility manifests in the digital age, where it often takes on a performative – and at times even tyrannical – quality. Individuals and institutions alike may seek to control public opinion, use visibility as a tool of influence or manipulate their image to gain recognition or power. On social media platforms, for instance, individuals create content, share personal details and actively construct public personas – all of which can be seen as modern expressions of the will to visibility. In this context, visibility is not simply a matter of physical presence or passive self-exhibition; it is the outcome of deliberate self-presentation – an active process of crafting and maintaining a personal narrative that others can witness, respond to and potentially validate.

The will to visibility, therefore, encompasses not only the desire to be seen but also the desire to *control* the terms of that visibility – a dynamic that can be both empowering and oppressive. Political leaders or celebrities often engage in performative publicness, carefully managing their public image to assert control, authority and power. Likewise, individuals increasingly curate their online presence through meticulously crafted posts, projecting idealised versions of themselves. Yet this drive for visibility can become destructive when it morphs into a compulsive need for constant attention or validation, fostering a toxic relationship with public exposure. This mirrors the cruelty and egotism that Arendt associates with the will to power: The unchecked pursuit of visibility may ultimately lead to self-destruction and societal harm.

What was once seen as a distortion of Enlightenment ideals of reason-based publicness has now become the new normal on social media platforms. Tönnies argued that the 'organic will', rooted in pre-rational (traditional, emotional) elements of human nature, was historically supplanted by the 'reflexive will', characterised by rational deliberation. Yet because forms of reflexive will are essentially rationalised versions of the organic will, the former remains dependent on the latter – often enabling manipulative and oppressive expressions of visibility to take precedence over reasoned discourse.

With the rise of ubiquitous communification public space has been technologically, economically and culturally democratised to the point where everyone and everything is allowed – and even expected – to appear in the public realm.[2] Communification has not only significantly increased access to this newly created virtual public space but has also transformed the nature of publicness and the purposes of publicity. Representative publicness now finds its modern counterpart in digital platform environments, where performative publicness thrives. Within the framework of contractual arrangements that govern access to visibility, achieving visibility has become the shared goal of both corporate and individual wills to visibility.

By privatising publicness and publicising privacy, platforms wield disproportionate control over communication infrastructures and user experiences, eroding trust in the authenticity of interactions and the fairness of discourse. The privatisation of publicness undermines the ideal of an open, democratic public sphere by concentrating discursive power in the hands of a few dominant tech corporations. Simultaneously, the publicisation of privacy discourages authentic engagement, as individuals become increasingly habituated to performative self-presentation. These dynamics echo historical practices of exclusivity and public spectacle – practices deeply inscribed in the evolving

---

2 Interestingly, while introducing *The Human Condition* (1958) with references to the major technological breakthroughs of the time – the first atomic explosions, which she saw as marking the birth of 'the modern world', and the launch of Sputnik 1 in 1957, the first artificial Earth satellite – and while extensively drawing on the ancient Greek *polis* to exemplify her notion of 'the public realm', Arendt completely ignores the media. Neither the press nor radio nor television is mentioned even once in the book.

genealogy of publicness – that have profoundly shaped the conditions under which gig publics emerge and operate.

From Print to Platform: The Evolution of Publics

Under such conditions, the process of forming public opinion is shifting towards regulated will formation, with the *gig public* emerging as its central actor. Gig publics are hosted on private platforms, meaning the very infrastructure of public discourse is entirely owned and operated by private corporations. Unlike traditional public spaces, which were governed by laws and norms designed to ensure inclusivity, equality and fairness, these digital environments are regulated by terms and conditions set through agreements between users, creators and platforms, tailored primarily to protect corporate interests.

As previously noted, the term *gig public* should not be understood in a normative sense, as denoting a 'special type of public', as is often implied by the adjectival modifiers common in contemporary academic discussions of (counter)publics and the public sphere. Rather, it serves as an analytical and structural concept that captures the *generic transformation of the public* under the conditions of surveillance capitalism. This transformation is driven by a surveillance economy powered by artificial intelligence, where large language models (LLMs) enable the purposeful manipulation of habitual behaviour, shaping and directing attention and engagement. These processes are facilitated by digital platforms that contractualise public discourse in a manner analogous to gig work. Through the pervasive deployment of AI and algorithmic technologies, the surveillance economy radically reshapes the contours and operations of publics in the contemporary digital age.

This complex interweaving of discursive processes of public opinion formation with traditional habitual and contractual relationships under surveillance capitalism presents a critical systemic challenge. This challenge arises from the fusion of three ostensibly incompatible forms of social will, as delineated by Tönnies: habits, contracts and public opinion – a fusion that materialises in the digital configuration of the gig public.

In a normative or 'pure theoretical' framework of Tönnies' system of elementary and complex forms of social will, the concepts of public and public opinion remain 'untainted' by the structural influences of legislative governance (the state), contractual exchange (the economy) and communal customs (habitual life). However, while this theoretical view separates public opinion from other forms of social will, in practice, public opinion is never fully isolated from the dynamics of political, economic and social structures. Rather, various expressions of social will are inherently 'mutually related and pass into each other' (Tönnies 1922, 228).

In *Gesellschaft* – where economic life is governed by *convention* and political life by *legislation* – 'public opinion refers primarily to the ethical (and in connection with this: the aesthetic) side of common life', yet it remains inherently interconnected with both convention and legislation (ibid., 229). In the contemporary context of communification and surveillance capitalism, this traditional interplay of ingrained habits, contractual frameworks and fragmented attempts at reasoned discourse has been reshaped and intensified, giving rise to what I call the gig public – a formation characterised by habitual, contractual and reasoned dimensions of engagement.

While gig publics hold the potential to discursively foster inclusivity and connectivity, their entanglement with profit-driven imperatives often leads to the marginalisation of dissent and the erosion of critical engagement. Like the *bourgeois public* and *proletarian public*, the gig public represents a *transitory* historical formation, emerging in the era of communification as a result of unmet conditions that hinder the realisation of the normative and epistemic idealisations of the public and publicness under surveillance capitalism.

Empirically, and in contrast to the idealised concept of publicness in normative theory, the actual public includes controversial and even irrational views and values, along with their proponents. These actors are granted access to communication channels, information and public discussion not through epistemic merit, but through contractual arrangements with internet content and service providers – even when they fail to meet the normative standards traditionally associated with publicness.

Of the six components of publicness outlined in my VARMIL scheme (Splichal 2022) and briefly presented in the introductory chapter – visibility, access, reflexivity, mediativity, influence and legitimisation – two in particular, *reflexivity* and *mediativity*, are critically undermined by the intrinsic nature of performative publicness. Reflexivity entails the capacity to critically examine one's own views and their epistemic foundations, fostering self-awareness and critical evaluation of one's beliefs. Mediativity, on the other hand, focuses on the mediating function of public communication, emphasising the importance of bridging epistemic distances between interlocutors in the public sphere based on the criticisability of their claims. The erosion of these two dimensions – discursive reflexivity and mediativity – undermines the deliberative quality of public engagement, accelerating fragmentation, polarisation and the dominance of affectively charged performative communication.

The gig public exemplifies the contractual form of will formation, though not in the Enlightenment sense of the social contract, which assumes that legitimate social and political institutions are founded on the reasoned consent of free and equal individuals. Unlike the normative universality of the social contract, the gig public operates through asymmetrical, often opaque agreements between users and platforms – contracts that are typically unilateral, non-negotiable and deeply intertwined with habitual platform usage. These are not collective compacts but clickwrap arrangements embedded in algorithmic architectures, prioritising commercial imperatives over deliberative ideals.

Consequently, the ethical core of publicness – anchored in collective deliberation and normative reason – is displaced by individualised, affectively driven interactions governed by platform-defined norms. By privileging platform contracts and subordinating democratic deliberation to proprietary logic, the gig public undermines the reciprocal accountability between political authority and the public that Kant deemed essential for the formation of a reasoned public.

As Kant argued, mutual accountability between governance and public opinion ensures the stability and efficacy of democratic processes. Transparency and justice in political decision-making are necessary to foster public trust, while the public, in turn, must uphold the rule of law and engage actively in democratic deliberation to sustain the legitimacy and integrity of institutional frameworks. The absence of these foundational elements raises critical questions about the validity and viability of the modern social contract – the normative foundation underpinning capitalist democracies, the ethical principles guiding human action and the mechanisms legitimating political authority. These are not merely ideal constructs but infrastructural conditions of publicness (Splichal 2022). The formation and operation of the gig public – mediated by algorithmic environments and shaped by corporate imperatives – destabilise these conditions, transforming the conditions under which accountability, transparency and collective engagement are meant to be realised.

Ever since the Enlightenment, publicness and the public have functioned more as counterfactual ideals than a lived reality. The conceptualisation of the 'reasoned public' was always tethered to Enlightenment rationalism and liberal elitism, privileging educated, property-owning, predominantly male citizens. Despite its rhetorical commitment to inclusivity and equality, the formation of the bourgeois public was inherently constrained by entrenched class, gender and racial hierarchies. At its core, the bourgeois public was less a universal forum for rational debate than a selective space for the articulation of dominant interests through stylised deliberation.

Yet paradoxically, the contemporary gig public, when compared to the historically transcended bourgeois public, may exhibit even less autonomy and self-determination than its bourgeois predecessor. Although the latter

was shaped by class-specific norms and exclusions, the conventions governing early reading publics – predominantly composed of bourgeois men – and
coffeehouse debates – however commercial in form – did not fully negate
the possibility of relatively autonomous deliberation. In contrast, today's gig
publics are increasingly formed through opaque, asymmetrical contractual
relationships and algorithmic filtering, which profoundly constrain the conditions under which communicative autonomy can be exercised.

Even when the class and gender exclusions of early bourgeois publics are
set aside, the commercial-contractual conventions that governed early reading publics arguably posed fewer systemic challenges to the nature and function of publicness than those facing today's gig publics. While embedded in
market logics, these early publics still retained a degree of deliberative coherence and structural intelligibility. Yet even then, critical voices emerged to
warn of the corrosive effects of media commodification.

Tönnies (1922, 183–187) explicitly criticised the harmful 'side effects' of
press commercialisation, which he believed distorted public opinion and
undermined its normative functions. He called for a radical reform of the
press to restore its ethical foundations. Similarly, Sorokin (1941/1992, 135)
warned of the erosion of genuine public opinion under the weight of corporate and factional interests. He observed the rise of 'pseudo-public opinions of
various factions' engineered by 'unscrupulous pressure groups' who manipulated ethics for personal gain. For Sorokin (1957/1970, 699), this trend signalled the collapse of a shared moral orientation and the weakening of what
he envisioned as a 'world conscience'.

In today's era of surveillance capitalism, however, tendencies once regarded
as undesirable or latent in public opinion formation have evolved into integral components of the public, giving rise to AI-driven epistemic enclaves.
Biases, preferences and behaviours previously deemed irrelevant or marginal
are now systematically harnessed and amplified by algorithms, segmenting
individuals into pre-packaged, tailored and siloed information bubbles. By
aggregating vast datasets on users' past and predicted behaviours, emotional
responses and other datafied characteristics – both of individuals and the
groups they are digitally connected to – AI systems actively shape the boundaries and dynamics of the gig public.

Yet, contractual dynamics within the public retain several elements traditionally associated with its theoretical (normative) conceptualisation.
Communicative actions constitutive of the public typically have a finite dura-
tion, oscillating between habitual/customary practices and more formal
contractual arrangements marked by voluntary participation, distinct from
mandatory relationships. Members of the gig public still engage as strangers in collective discourse. However, the widespread prevalence of online

contractual relations introduces changes that significantly impede the capacity of (potential) publics to generate public opinion as an expression of the *general will* through *reasoned debate.*

Cohesion within these online networks is often driven by pragmatic and utilitarian self-interests, with individuals primarily focused on their own concerns and offering minimal intellectual input while showing limited regard for the well-being, efforts, aspirations and values of others. This fosters a fragmented, transactional mode of interaction, exemplified by the performative unity of a collective 'we' in gig publics. Often, this unity is orchestrated by founding 'contractors', who may also control the recommendation algorithms that help constitute gig publics, thus encouraging the formation of opinion enclaves.

In sociological terms, the nature of the public has undergone a dramatic transformation, evolving from the stable, collective structures of the newspaper era to the fragmented, ephemeral forms of the gig public in the digital age. In the reasoned public, reason is assumed to prevail over the will to visibility, as reflexive will is integrated into the thought process. Conversely, in the gig public, the will to visibility dominates reason, much as natural will governs the elements of thought as part of an instinctive process. This shift reflects profound changes in how people connect, interact and participate in public discourse – changes driven by technological advancements, the rise of surveillance capitalism and broader changes in the formation and conceptualisation of publicness and the public.

In the newspaper era, publics were formed around the shared experience of reading newspapers, which functioned as central institutions – 'organs' – of the public. Their stability stemmed from the institutional and technological constraints of newspapers – fixed publication schedules, standardised reporting formats, professional editorial oversight and a limited number of competing newspapers. People were symbolically connected through the shared act of reading and the awareness that others were simultaneously consuming the same content. The collective experience of reading a daily or weekly newspaper fostered a sense of connection and commonality among readers, even though – as Tarde wrote – they were physically dispersed over a vast territory, not seeing or hearing each other, but sitting at home and reading the same newspaper. He argued that this 'bond' among people 'lies in their simultaneous conviction or passion and in their awareness of sharing at the same time an idea or a wish with a great number of other men. It suffices for a man to know this, even without seeing these others, to be influenced by them *en masse*' (1901/2003, 9).

Reading publics were shaped by the regular rhythms of daily or weekly newspaper publishing. As gatekeepers of information, newspapers played a

pivotal role in controlling the flow of news stories and directing public attention and defining the contours of public discourse. While access to newspapers and to participation in publics was limited by socio-economic and
cultural barriers that excluded marginalised groups and large segments of the
proletariat, newspapers nonetheless provided a relatively uniform national
platform for discussion and debate, fostering civic engagement and the construction of collective identities. Public opinion in this era – while 'gaseous'
or 'fluid', as Tönnies described it – was nonetheless anchored in a sense of
representing a broad spectrum of society and collective social recognition,
aspiring to nourish rational-critical conversation.

   The 'conversation' of readers with newspapers was considered just
as important for the formation of public opinion as their interpersonal
exchanges. Newspapers helped create a public by stimulating face-to-face
dialogue, which, in turn, influenced the direction, strength and intensity of
public opinion. The frequency, boldness and collective dynamics of these
conversations influenced the strength, direction and intensity of public
opinion (Tarde 1901, 72). The study of conversation later became central in
the 'pioneering analysis of the public by the "Chicago School"' (Gouldner
1976, 97). Similarly to Tarde, Dewey (1927/1946, 219) argued that 'word of
mouth from one to another in the communications of the local community
[...] gives reality to public opinion'. The foundational and transformative
potential of conversation in shaping the public and public opinion became
a central theme in discussions about reimagining publicness in the early
visions of the Internet, which was initially believed to offer unprecedented
possibilities for democratic dialogue. Alongside these optimistic visions, the
idea of the 'public sphere' emerged in the 1980s. However, as subsequent
developments have shown, these hopes for a democratic-conversational
transformation of publicness have proven both technologically and politically naïve.

   Although newspapers were embedded in the capitalist economy from the
very beginning, their role as gatekeepers of information afforded them a
degree of autonomy and credibility, allowing them to frame public discourse
as a democratic good rather than merely a commercial product. Writing during the emergence of radio, Brecht envisioned a technological revolution that
would socialise communication – or, failing that, spark a social revolution
to achieve the same. Yet, under the dominance of capital and commercial
imperatives, subsequent media developments facilitated the fragmentation
of audiences, the prioritisation of entertainment over deliberation and the
'refeudalization of the public sphere', as Habermas described it. The rise of
digital platforms has effectively consummated this process, fundamentally
altering the structure and dynamics of publics.

Gig publics operate on a technological and institutional foundation that differs sharply from that of reading publics. Rather than being anchored by the authority and editorial gatekeeping of newspapers, they are governed by algorithms that prioritise visibility, attention and profitability. Social media platforms, streaming services and search engines generate personalised, ephemeral spaces – often echo chambers – where individuals engage with content tailored to their preferences. The algorithms that control user engagement and content dissemination tend to reinforce existing biases and suppress diversity in public discourse. As users interact within increasingly siloed communities, opportunities for cross-cutting dialogue diminish, weakening the basis for collective understanding and shared democratic ideals. This privatised and decentralised infrastructure undermines the development of shared narratives and a lasting collective consciousness, instead fostering fleeting, performative forms of public communication.

In contrast to the structured and relatively coherent reading publics of the newspaper era, gig publics are fluid, fragmented and constantly in flux. Publicness in this context is no longer mediated through shared reading and deliberation but through highly individualised and performative acts of creating visibility, such as simple social media posts, participation in trending topics or momentary online campaigns. These publics form and dissolve rapidly, driven by virality, platform dynamics and algorithmic mediation. Unlike the representation of shared experiences in newspaper publics, gig publics are fragmented into partly overlapping micro-collectivities, where the primary 'bond' emerges not through socially constructed dialogue but through algorithmically curated, personalised interactions.

This shift from newspaper-reading publics to gig publics carries profound implications for civic engagement and democratic representation. The cohesive structure of reading publics enabled a degree of shared representation, collective identity and sustained societal impact. By contrast, gig publics are fragmented and increasingly performative, posing serious challenges for fostering an inclusive public sphere. These dynamics privilege performative expressions aimed at enhancing individual visibility and accruing social capital, rather than fostering substantive dialogue or collective action oriented towards 'the consequences of acts which are so important as to need control, whether by inhibition or by promotion' (Dewey 1927/1946, 15).

One of the most striking characteristics of gig publics is their dynamism. Unlike the relative stability and rhythm of newspaper-based publics, gig publics are marked by constant flux, with attention moving rapidly from one topic, trend or controversy to another. While this volatility can enable swift mobilisation around specific events or urgent issues, it also hinders the capacity for sustained public debate on complex or controversial topics with significant long-term societal consequences. Without continuity or cohesion, it becomes difficult to maintain the deliberative focus necessary to address issues that require prolonged civic engagement and deliberation.

Despite these limitations, gig publics are not without democratic potential. Their fluid and modular nature can enable the inclusion of diverse social groups and amplify voices historically marginalised in traditional public forums. Digital platforms, for all their constraints, provide new opportunities for grassroots organising, transnational activism and networked collaboration. Yet, the capacity of gig publics to foster meaningful engagement remains conditional. It hinges on the extent to which we can confront and transform the structural and technological logics that commodify participation, extract attention as a resource and subordinate civic discourse to the imperatives of platform profitability.

'Hop-on-Hop-off' Discursive Sightseeing: Roaming the Landscapes of Publicness

The gig public can be metaphorically compared to the flexibility, episodic nature and convenience of *hop-on-hop-off* sightseeing bus tours. Just as tourists board and disembark at curated points of interest, engaging with specific suggested destinations without committing to the full journey, individuals in gig publics engage selectively with topics, platforms or digital events that capture their attention, participating briefly before moving on without considering their broader public relevance.

This metaphor highlights the interplay between user agency and the structural influence of platform design in shaping gig public engagement. Much like passengers on a hop-on-hop-off tour, members of the gig public occasionally encounter one another online within predefined parameters, choosing their level of engagement. Despite this apparent autonomy, however, their involvement is shaped – and often constrained – by habitual practices, contractual arrangements and algorithmic curation of content, all of which dictate the scope and direction of user interactions, limiting opportunities for deeper exploration and dialogue.

Habits, customs and conventions have always played a significant role in the formation of publics and public opinion, despite being relatively neglected in much public sphere theorisation. However, the algorithmisation of discourse within integrated public–private digital communication networks has intensified the longstanding contradictions between the normative ideals of publicness and the practical conditions under which public opinion is formed. Similar to tourist experiences that prioritise instant convenience over immersive exploration, accessibility and immediacy are favoured in the gig public at the expense of sustained engagement and collective deliberation. The journey is fragmented, lacking a cohesive narrative and shared 'destination,' reflecting the transient and disconnected nature of participation in the gig public. Much like the limited interaction among passengers with diverse social and cultural backgrounds and interests on a hop-on-hop-off tour – who, despite partially sharing the same journey, remain isolated – members of the gig public coexist on the same platform but often remain alienated within algorithmically curated epistemic enclaves.

While there are parallels between a 'hop-on-hop-off' public and a normatively conceptualised reasoned public – such as an emphasis on access, inclusivity, visibility, participation and transience – the differences across these and other dimensions of publicness are equally significant. A closer examination of these distinctions reveals the evolving nature of publicness in mediated public–private spaces.

Accessibility and Inclusivity. Like hop-on-hop-off tours that cater to a wide range of users by offering various easily accessible packages, the gig public is composed of diverse individuals. Digital platforms with low thresholds of access make it easy for people from a range of demographic, professional and cultural backgrounds, and with varied value orientations, to 'hop on', become visible and share their perspectives. Just as hop-on-hop-off tours stop at multiple points of interest, the gig public offers a multitude of communicative entry points – ranging from niche forums to large-scale social media platforms – where users can engage with topics that capture their interest or align with their passions.

However, even though platforms are technically open to all in principle, private corporations often control this virtual space, setting the rules for participation that can inadvertently or intentionally exclude certain voices. Content moderation and fact-checking policies, embedded in recommendation algorithms, prioritise some content over others, subtly shaping which voices are amplified or suppressed under the guise of enforcing community standards.[3] This dynamic can disproportionately silence marginalised groups, narrowing the range of available perspectives and leading to epistemic enclaves.

---

3 In early 2025, Meta corporation owner, Zuckerberg – like Musk before him on his X network – announced the abolition of fact-checking and restrictions on hate speech on Facebook and Instagram, claiming that they were politically biased censorship interfering with freedom of expression. This decision was made to curry favour with President Trump, but its consequences are much more far-reaching, as it gives far-right activists a free rein to routinely spread lies, distortions and hate speech on social media.

Moreover, the sheer volume of participants and information in the gig public can overwhelm users, making it difficult for inclusivity alone to translate into meaningful engagement. Dominant voices, or the sheer cacophony of voices, often drown out a genuine diversity of voices – even if they are present – thus limiting their impact on public discourse.

The See All the Sights in a Day maxim captures a defining dynamic of participation in gig publics. The gig public is inherently fluid, characterised by fleeting engagement rather than sustained deliberation or clear resolutions. Like fleeting visits of tourists exploring a city's attractions, participants in this public can 'hop on' and 'hop off' various digital platforms, topics or discussions at will – often in quick succession or even simultaneously – sampling content rather than engaging deeply. While gig publics may be widely open and accessible, the nature of participation is superficial and transient, with users entering for a short visit and then rushing towards the next 'destination' to visit as many as possible. The vast number of available 'routes' and 'stops' within the gig public disperses participants across segregated spaces, limiting their exposure to diverse viewpoints and reducing the potential for collective deliberation.

In contrast to traditionally conceptualised publics – where participation is rooted in in-depth attention, reflexive reasoning and a shared commitment to collective goals – the gig public is marked by diffuse attention and episodic interactions, driven by personal convenience and immediate gratification. Its transient nature, in which individuals are continually diverted from critical discourse by shifting topics, fleeting conversations and digital distractions, not only undermines the depth of deliberation but also weakens the potential for meaningful social bonds. As a result, the emergence of collective opinion – the ultimate 'destination' of a normatively conceptualised public – is significantly impeded.

I Was Here! The song by American singer Beyoncé, in which she declares, 'I was here [...] I will leave my mark so everyone will know I was here', serves as a poignant metaphor for the ethos of the gig public, encapsulating the will to visibility that drives much of online engagement. Unlike Beyoncé's expression of a desire to leave a lasting legacy, members of the gig public exhibit a 'tourist mentality,' seeking to document or mark their fleeting presence in digital spaces. Just as tourists briefly visiting a landmark snap a photo to share with family and friends before moving on, members of the gig public interact with digital platforms to make their presence and attitudes visible through status updates, posts, selfies, blogs, vlogs or likes. The desire to leave a trace and validate one's momentary participation is a defining trait of engagement within the gig public.

In essence, while the desire of gig public members to 'leave a mark' reflects a natural human impulse for recognition, it also underscores the need to reimagine how we engage with one another in public–private digital spaces. Moving beyond the tourist mentality towards a more committed, reflexive mode of communication is essential to restoring the public's potential for reasoned democratic deliberation.

Algorithm-Guided 'Sightseeing' in gig publics is a commodified service defined by platform contracts strategically engineered to maximise engagement and capture attention. Recommendation algorithms play a central role in this 'tourist experience': They function as algorithmic 'tour guides', promoting a 'tourist mentality' of fleeting involvement by steering users towards the most 'popular' or 'attractive' stops, tailored to their calculated habits and inferred interests. These algorithms define a 'path' based on collective trends, individual preferences and marketing opportunities, subtly directing users towards pre-selected destinations. Much like a tour itinerary that highlights specific attractions, algorithms prioritise content based on users' habitual interactions. However, unlike hop-on-hop-off tours with clearly mapped, transparent routes, algorithmic journeys are deceptively curated to appear personalised while remaining fundamentally preconfigured – an emblematic feature of gig publics.

While passengers on a sightseeing bus can disembark and explore freely, algorithms often provide only the illusion of choice. Users are nudged towards content that reinforces their existing behaviours and preferences, creating feedback loops that confine their digital exploration. This curated journey offers the comfort of routine and habitual action but at the same time restricts opportunities for genuine discovery and serendipitous encounters.

To some extent, algorithm-guided 'sightseeing' incorporates elements of serendipity – exposing users to unfamiliar content they might not have encountered otherwise – as important triggers to foster curiosity and user engagement. By introducing users to new ideas and diverse perspectives, 'serendipitous' recommendations can move them beyond existing biases, reinforce a broader range of viewpoints and even help disrupt filter bubbles (Stitini et al. 2023). However, the efficacy of these mechanisms is constrained by the algorithm's architecture, the user's ingrained habits and the commercial priorities of platform operators. Rather than encouraging users to engage with content that has significant long-term implications for the common good, algorithmic curation confines them to controlled itineraries that reinforce attention-driven habitual behaviours.

Much like circular hop-on-hop-off tourist bus tours, the gig public often leaves participants without a clear sense of purpose or destination of the discursive journey. What may initially seem like a journey of discovery and dialogue frequently devolves into a fragmented experience, marked by shallow, repetitive and isolated interactions with content that merely validates

pre-existing beliefs. This habitual behaviour – scrolling through feeds, react-
ing to trends, responding to notifications – nurtures a 'scrolling culture' that
privileges superficial browsing and passive consumption of information.

Personal Choice and Habitual Commitment. In the short term, participants are
not bound by a predetermined route; instead, they curate their engagement
based on curiosity or convenience. The gig public enables users to navigate
a variety of 'stops' in the digital realm. This characteristic aligns with the
broader ethos of the Internet, where hyperlinked structures – online messages
and content interconnected through links – and algorithmic recommendations encourage lateral exploration. The absence of a fixed path fosters a sense
of spontaneity and openness, allowing participants to explore diverse sites or
perspectives without long-term commitments. This short-term engagement
often generates vibrant discussions, characterised by immediacy, novelty and
variety.

In the long term, however, the patterns of engagement within the gig
public may reveal considerable constraints. Despite the initial appearance
of free exploration, participants' choices are often shaped and channelled by
algorithmic influences, habitual behaviours and platform-specific dynamics.
Algorithms prioritise certain types of content based on users' previous interactions, gradually narrowing the range of visible 'stops' and steering participants towards more predictable and less diverse pathways. This process,
commonly referred to as the formation of echo chambers or filter bubbles,
reduces exposure to novel ideas and dissenting opinions, thereby undermining the very freedom and variety that characterise the gig public's short-term
appeal.

The long-term effects of the gig public's dynamics thus create a paradox:
While it promotes exploration and personal choice in the short term, its
longer-term tendencies towards algorithmic steering and habitual engagement challenge the ideals of an open, inclusive and dynamic public sphere.
Although the hop-on-hop-off nature of the gig public accommodates a diverse
range of participants and appears to grant them freedom, this flexibility is
often superficial. It ultimately complicates collective will-formation and compromises the integrity of public discourse. As a result, the ephemerality and
segmentation of gig publics hinder the development of a cohesive, empowered
public capable of holding authorities accountable and driving social change.

The Structural Immaturity of the Gig Public: The Habitual, Contractual and Algorithmic Enclosure of Reason

In essence, the conditions of modern public–private communication networks, within which the gig public is emerging, bear striking similarities to

the early commercialisation of newspapers – a development Marx harshly criticised. Just as printing technology was pivotal to the rise of the early bourgeois public, computer-mediated communication technologies and artificial intelligence are crucial to the formation of the modern gig public.

Marx's normative defence of press freedom was not primarily motivated by granting liberty *to the press* (e.g., newspapers) per se, but rather *to citizens* – as their right and as a realisation of universal freedom. As he wrote, 'What I cannot be for others, I am not for myself and cannot be for myself' (1842/1974, 73). In his view, newspapers should serve as the vital link between the individual and society, acting as a mirror through which the people can see and examine themselves; a transformative force that turns material struggles into intellectual and cultural ones; an embodiment of a people's trust in itself; and an omnipresent, inspiring spirit that reflects and shapes the ideal world (ibid., 60–61). The press, he asserted, is 'the product of public opinion [that], at the same time, also produces public opinion' (Marx 1843/1974, 189–190).

Even more than condemning state censorship, Marx warned against the subjugation of the press to market forces – a dynamic that reduces press freedom to a mere subset of commercial freedom. He argued that the freedom of the press entails that it should not function as a business in the first place. Justifying press freedom by equating it with entrepreneurial freedom – though seemingly appealing and effective at first glance – would, in his view, mean defending it while simultaneously undermining it; it threatens it more than it defends it.

Marx's warning now appears as a prophetic critique of the evolving dynamics of media discourse that have led to the emergence of the gig public. For Marx, the fundamental purpose of democratic freedom is compromised when it becomes merely a tool for advancing commercial interests. He drew a sharp distinction between journalism as a public, democratic practice and the press as a profit-driven enterprise. While he acknowledged that writers must earn money in order to live and write, he was unequivocally opposed to the idea that they should live and write in order to make money.

This critique gains renewed relevance in today's digital landscape, where the commodification of communication prioritises profit over the democratic principles of public discourse. Algorithmically driven communication on digital platforms, on the one hand, and the rise of the will to visibility, on the other, reproduce contradictions that Marx had already identified at the early age of print. Commercial imperatives – now enforced and amplified by algorithms – entangle gig publics in a relentless cycle of generating the habitualised and contractualised will to visibility, overshadowing ideals of democratic public engagement.

Marx's critique of the press highlights how contractual commercial relation-ships subordinate public communication to entrepreneurial freedom, turning democratic practices into tradable commodities. In the gig public, habitual relationships – subtly yet significantly tied to business contracts – achieve a similar effect. These relationships tether users to repetitive, routinised and automatic behaviours that gradually come to natural and self-evident. Users become enmeshed in a vicious cycle of platform-driven behaviour: On the one hand, they are 'products' of the commercial strategies of digital corpora-tions; on the other, they are unwittingly complicit in enacting and reinforcing these very entrepreneurial agendas.

Contractual relationships further reinforce this trend of commodification by standardising and formalising interactions among users, creators and platforms into socially entrenched conventions, often requiring users to cede their rights in exchange for access to digital content and services. The interplay of these habit-ual and contractual frameworks shapes both individual discursive agency and institutional control within integrated public–private communication networks. Together, these dynamics constitute the backbone of the gig public, where per-sonal engagement and structural regulation coalesce, shaping the nature of digital interaction and its far-reaching implications for public discourse.

AI and recommendation algorithms serve as a bridge between discursive participation, habitual behaviour and contractual relationships – the three forms of will formation constitutive of publicness – by amplifying and harmo-nising their effects. In this process, user engagement and platform influence reinforce one another. AI-driven algorithms leverage habitual engagement by analysing data derived from user behaviours to refine and personalise con-tent delivery, operating within the contractual frameworks that govern data usage, content visibility and platform control.

The contractual relationships in the gig public are governed by explicit and implicit terms and conditions that users are effectively compelled to accept in order to access privately owned digital platforms. Often buried in lengthy, detailed and hard-to-read terms of service documents, these conditions regu-late access to communication channels, establish rules for participation, and define the stakes of user engagement.[4] By consenting to these terms, users relinquish significant control over their engagement to platform owners, who

---

4 For example, the Facebook Terms of Service – the main document defining who can use Facebook, how it can be used, what permissions users grant to the parent company Meta, and other terms of use – which users agree to by accessing or using the platform, exceeds 5,600 words. However, many additional terms and policies apply to Facebook users, specified in other documents that users are invited to read, such as the commer-cial terms, cookies policy, 'no ads' terms and many others. The total length of all these additional documents combined could range from 5,500 to 12,000 words.

enforce policies on content moderation, algorithmic visibility and data collection – policies that profoundly influence how individuals interact with digital
platforms and with each other.

For content creators, their contractual relationship with digital platforms
–governing ad revenues, sponsorships and content monetisation – transforms
their co-creation of performative publicness into a form of largely unpaid gig
work. By publicising aspects of their private lives, these individuals exercise
their will to visibility. Occasionally, this instrumental publicity provides a
modest income in exchange for the alienation of their privacy, with platform
algorithms determining both visibility and remuneration based on the level
of attention their content receives.

The habitualisation of individual engagement in the gig public transforms private behaviours into public acts. Digital platforms encourage users
to continually, whether voluntarily or unknowingly, expose aspects of their
private lives and relinquish personal data in exchange for access, visibility
and occasional commercial rewards. Personal preferences, interests and
intimate moments are shared publicly as part of users' ongoing interaction
with these platforms. Over time, daily recurring activities – such as scrolling
through social media feeds, liking posts, following accounts, commenting on
trending topics and sharing personal content – are reinforced by dopamine-
driven feedback mechanisms designed by platforms, eventually solidifying
into ingrained habits. Additional features, such as popular hashtags, gami-
fied interactions and recommendations to join specific online groups, further
embed users into the habit-forming rhythm of platform engagement. These
'prefabricated rules' advance shallow, performative engagement, normalising
fragmented and transient interactions into routine and predictable performances of gig publics.

Although habitual relationships may appear voluntary, they are often
shaped by deliberate platform design and algorithmic nudges aligned with
commercial imperatives. Unlike contractual conventions that overtly subordinate users to entrepreneurial freedom, habitual relationships subtly redirect user agency to serve platform agendas. This indirect subordination arises
through habituation: a process by which individuals internalise platform
logics and routines. Repetitive behaviours, fostered by habitual attachment
to platforms, contribute to the commodification of public discourse – often
without the explicit consent or awareness of users, who increasingly function
as 'produsers': both producers and consumers of content. Through the intertwining of habitual and contractual relationships, the gig public becomes
subject to the structural market pressures that restrict individual autonomy
to ensure the profitability of platform capitalism. Habituation thus becomes a
mechanism of surveillance that conceals the economic structures underlying

it, creating an illusion of autonomy while ultimately reinforcing corporate priorities.

The interplay between communicative agency, habitual and contractual relationships and algorithmic governance profoundly shapes the dynamics of the gig public. Habitual platform use normalises the passive acceptance of contractual terms, often without critical reflection. These contracts, which define the operation of recommendation algorithms and content curation protocols, subsequently influence user habits. This interdependence creates a vicious cycle of contractual and habitual dependence on platforms. On one hand, habitual engagement discourages critical examination of exploitative agreements and limits demands for transparency and accountability. On the other hand, contractual mechanisms reinforce and structure these very habits, stabilising power asymmetries in favour of platforms, which wield disproportionate control over information flows, discourse moderation and the architecture of engagement.

At the heart of these transactional relationships – both habitual and contractual – lies the commodification of users' future attention and behavioural or decisional intentions, exchanged for access to the production and consumption of online content. With the integration of large language models (LLMs), these personalised transactions – whether sharing private moments in exchange for greater visibility and attention or providing intention-signalling personal data and preferences for cheaper or more comprehensive access – enable platforms to anticipate and steer user behaviours based on their habits and projected intentions ('future habits'). In this way, platforms commodify not only user attention but also user intention.

Drawing on data extracted from past behaviours, algorithms can calculate users' probable future intentions – intentions of which users are neither aware nor have access to, let alone control over, the algorithmic processes or the data used to generate such forecasts. Users thereby become 'the sources of surveillance capitalism's crucial surplus: the objects of a technologically advanced and increasingly inescapable raw-material-extraction operation' (Zuboff 2019, 88). Unwittingly, they sustain a surveillance economy that commodifies their attention and behaviour, allowing corporations to exploit these 'raw materials' for profit, while users remain at the mercy of opaque algorithmic systems and their consequences.

A key long-term consequence of these habitual-contractual dynamics is the transformation of the gig public into *epistemic enclaves*. Yet the problem of gig publics evolving into opinion enclaves transcends the role of algorithms alone. While algorithmic design plays a central role in shaping these enclaves within digital networks, a deeper issue lies in the psychological dynamics of human discourse – most evident in phenomena such as filter bubbles and echo chambers.

The gig public thrives on data-driven discursive interactions shaped by the behavioural data its members produce, fostering a sense of community, similarity and social interdependence. The tendency towards similarity among members of the public was already noted by Tarde, who described the commercialised public as 'deviant commercial clientele', unified by shared experience and consumption patterns. Long before the digital age, social psychology recognised how group behaviour amplifies the need for social validation and the fear of isolation, often producing conformist tendencies. Rooted in the psychological comfort of belonging, individuals frequently align their opinions or behaviours with the majority to secure inclusion – or, when identity is public, to avoid ostracism.

In the digital contexts of gig publics, these effects are exacerbated by the immediacy and visibility of social metrics used to quantify individual visibility, popularity and influence. Such metrics intensify social pressure to conform, prompting users to suppress dissenting or unpopular views in favour of group cohesion. This dynamic not only constrains genuine exchange but also narrows the diversity of perspectives and undermines the potential for critical discourse.

As individuals increasingly prioritise trendy 'alternative facts' and social media-driven, ad hoc opinions over critical, evidence-based reasoning, they risk overlooking substantial evidence and engaging with incomplete or misleading information. This flawed epistemic process shapes beliefs and opinions through a self-affirming feedback loop within epistemic enclaves, accelerating the spread of misinformation and normalising poor decision-making. It undermines the productive function of reducing cognitive dissonance by motivating individuals, exposed to the discomfort triggered by dissenting or conflicting beliefs, attitudes or values, to resolve these inconsistencies by modifying those 'cognitive elements', rather than indiscriminately rejecting them (Festinger 1957).

In contrast, epistemic enclaves 'resolve' dissonance pre-emptively by creating cognitive consonance in advance – without the user's awareness. This undermines the capacity for what might be termed the 'Kantian test': the reflexive act of evaluating one's own judgements from a universal standpoint to assess both their subjective coherence (for oneself) and their objective validity (for others). Isolated from opposing viewpoints, individuals become epistemically impoverished, lacking insight into others' opinions and the reasoning that supports them, which impedes their ability to consider alternative perspectives. Within enclaves governed by consensus and social affirmation, dissenting views are suppressed, critical thought is discouraged and collective misjudgements become more likely. These dynamics reinforce false beliefs, perpetuate misinformation and deepen societal polarisation.

The rise of the malignant spread of misinformation and disinformation, epistemic segregation and political polarisation, both online and in broader society, echoes the decline of traditional news media, especially newspapers, as well as the deprofessionalisation of journalism and the erosion of trust in journalistic institutions[5] – processes inherently linked to the formation of the gig public. These changes are critical, as early sociological conceptualisations of the public and public opinion were grounded in the role of newspapers as facilitators of truth, forums for deliberation and watchdogs holding power to account.[6] These functions, rooted in the habitual and implicit contractual relationship between newspapers and the reading public, were supposed to foster a shared commitment to informed public discourse. However, even at that time, scholars like Tönnies (1922, 201) expressed scepticism about journalism's capacity to consistently fulfil these ideals, observing: 'Untrue news often serves the interest of the person who disseminates it better than true news, and the concealment and suppression of true information may be preferentially beneficial.'

Despite such early warnings of ethical corruption in the newspaper industry, the public's reading culture endured through the rise of radio and television, substantially disrupted by the advent of social media. As social media

---

5 In late 2024, Elon Musk, CEO of Tesla and a senior adviser in Trump's White House in 2025, used his platform X (formerly Twitter) to declare traditional journalism obsolete, advocating instead for 'citizen journalism' as the future. He argued that news should be controlled 'by the people, for the people', dismissing legacy media as unreliable and urging political leaders to communicate directly on X rather than through professional journalists. Musk framed this shift as a move towards 'authenticity', claiming that mistakes in user-generated content prove its 'realness'. However, critics warn that Musk's vision undermines fact-checked, professional journalism, instead promoting unverified, emotionally driven narratives. His posts during the 2024 US elections accused mainstream media of dishonesty, encouraging users to post uncensored opinions on X as the sole source of truth. This stance risks amplifying misinformation, eroding public trust in reliable news and replacing informed discourse with unchecked bias – posing a long-term threat to democratic dialogue (https://x.com/elonmusk/status/1854206931256099056; https://x.com/ElonFactsX/status/1854162202472726756).

6 Following Musk's support for US President Trump's politics, Amazon Corporation and *Washington Post* owner Jeff Bezos, the world's wealthiest person, announced a 'significant shift' in the newspaper's opinion page editorial policy in an X post on February 26, 2025, 'We are going to be writing every day in support and defence of two pillars: personal liberties and free markets. We'll cover other topics too, of course, but viewpoints opposing those pillars will be left to be published by others […]. I'm confident that free markets and personal liberties are right for America. I also believe these viewpoints are underserved in the current market of ideas and news opinion. I'm excited for us together to fill that void' (https://x.com/jeffbezos/status/1894757287052362088?s=46).

platforms gained prominence, the proportion of citizens engaging with traditional news outlets – such as newspapers, television broadcasts and radio programmes – declined significantly. Social media increasingly became the preferred source for news consumption. Although the Internet was initially heralded as a catalyst for the advancement of journalism, the industry now faces a crisis of credibility and influence. Traditional media, particularly newspapers and magazines, have experienced a marked decline in both readership and frequency of use.[7]

Research links the closure of an increasing number of newspapers to alarming social trends, including declining civic engagement, lower voter

---

7 In the United States alone, approximately 2,200 local print newspapers shut down between 2005 and 2021. This decline has been mirrored in the workforce: from 2008 to 2020, the number of American newspaper journalists dropped by more than half (*The Washington Post* 2021). Compounding this trend, even the most popular digital news websites have experienced declining traffic (Lipka and Shearer 2023). A key factor behind this decline is the erosion of direct access news outlets have to their audiences, particularly younger users, as more people turn to third-party platforms and aggregators for news content.

In the European Union, TV remains the most widely used news channel, with 71 per cent of respondents in a 2023 study citing it as their primary source, followed by online press and news platforms (42 per cent), social media (37 per cent), radio (37 per cent) and printed press (21 per cent). While usage rates for all other media remained stable or saw slight declines from 2022 to 2023, social media platforms experienced an 11-percentage-point increase in users. However, daily readership of the printed press has declined sharply – from 37 per cent in 2012 to just 21 per cent in 2022.

Globally, direct access to news apps and websites is steadily declining as social media becomes the dominant gateway for online news consumption. A 2023 Reuters study spanning 46 countries found that 30 per cent of users now prefer social media for news, compared to just 22 per cent who rely on direct access to news apps or websites. This shift underscores social media's growing dominance over traditional news access methods (Newman et al. 2023). In the United States, one-third of the population listened to podcasts in 2023 with the intention of 'staying up to date on current events' (Pew 2023).

This shift is accompanied by a broader transformation in media consumption habits, with audiences moving away from in-depth reading of the written press towards quick, interactive and algorithm-driven engagement on digital platforms. The average time spent daily reading newspapers has decreased significantly. In the Asia-Pacific region, it dropped from 22 minutes in 2011 to just 9 minutes in 2018, with a continued downward trend – reaching only 5.2 minutes in Japan by 2023. Similarly, in the United States, the average time spent per visit to the top 50 daily newspapers websites fell to just under 1 minute and 30 seconds in 2022, marking a 43 per cent decline from 2014, when it exceeded 2 minutes and 30 seconds. By comparison, users spent significantly more time on other major platforms: 10 to 20 minutes on leading websites, up to 24.15 minutes on YouTube and 31.17 on WhatsApp (Pew 2023a; Statista 2025).

turnout (Stearns 2022), rising corruption in government and business sectors and growing political polarisation and nationalism (Reichel 2018). In this challenging digital environment, only a few well-established newspapers with strong brands and a robust online presence have managed to maintain or grow their readership. These outlets have adapted successfully to the digital age through innovation and strategic investment in development, while smaller and less capitalised publishers are finding it increasingly difficult to survive in a shrinking yet competitive newspaper market.

As social media platforms continue to grow in popularity and dominate daily information consumption, traditional news organisations are increasingly reliant on these platforms to establish habitual and contractual relationships with their readers, viewers and listeners. Moreover, the growing dependence of journalism on social media infrastructures and monetisation-driven business models is further weakening its role as the 'organ of the public'. In an effort to stay relevant, many media organisations now employ large teams of information professionals tasked with optimising content to maximise user engagement and drive traffic. This reliance on platform algorithms underscores journalism's precarious position – even among legacy outlets – where the pursuit of clicks, virality and profitability often comes at the expense of in-depth, critical reporting.

News outlets have become ever more dependent on global platform companies like Google, Meta and OpenAI, whose communications infrastructure, artificial intelligence and business models shape both content delivery and audience interaction.[8] Journalism, which has historically held a mandate to inform citizens, hold power to account and promote inclusive public debate, now faces systemic pressures that prioritise commercial success over democratic values and erode professional autonomy. As the field struggles to adapt to these tech-driven commercial transformations, the public risks becoming more vulnerable to disinformation, polarisation and corporate control. This

---

8 In 2024, the average Internet user worldwide spends over two hours and twenty minutes per day on social networking. In 2025, Facebook remains the world's most popular and widely used social media platform, with 3.07 billion monthly active users – representing 37 per cent of the global population. YouTube follows as the second most popular platform, with 2.53 billion users. Meanwhile, social networks focusing on short-form video content, such as Instagram and TikTo, and messaging applications like WhatsApp, Facebook Messenger and Telegram, are experiencing rapid growth, with some platforms expanding by more than 200 per cent per year. https://www.statista.com/statistics/433871/daily-social-media-usage-worldwide/#statisticContainer; https://www.statista.com/statistics/272014/global-social-networks-ranked-by-number-of-users/.

trend threatens the foundational ideals of transparency, accountability and informed deliberation – ideals essential to democratic societies.

These challenges extend beyond journalism's institutional crisis, affecting the restructuring of digital epistemic systems that now organise contemporary public discourse according to the logics of platform corporations. The resulting epistemic segregation erodes the foundations of independent critical thought and undermines the quality of public deliberation. In these often-fragmented virtual spaces, the structural difficulties of fostering rational engagement become glaringly apparent. A central manifestation of this epistemic segregation is the emergence of opinion enclaves, which both result from and perpetuate instrumental publicity. In contrast to the principles of both quality journalism and performative publicness, these enclaves serve primarily to defend the special interests of specific groups.

Such an environment forms the social breeding ground for the development of the gig public. In the Enlightenment tradition, newspapers – and journalists and editors as individuals – were seen as organs and representatives of public opinion, functioning simultaneously as its producers and products, as Marx observed. In contrast, today's social media platforms serve as technological, organisational and cultural infrastructures that enable, foster and organise the formation and functioning of gig publics – diversified and fragmented across various sectors and interests. This refiguration of publics echoes Robert Park's conception of public opinion as an objective phenomenon *sui generis*: external to any given individual, expressed and perceived differently by different people, rather than a general consensus or mere aggregate of private opinions.

The gig public represents a radical departure from the Enlightenment ideal of the public as a rational, critical entity engaged in open debate and self-reflection, ideally progressing towards universal enlightenment through reasoned discussion and the pursuit of truth. In contrast to this normatively conceptualised public, the gig public emerges as a digitally mediated, data-driven epistemic network constituted through interactive, performative and commodified discursive engagements. At its core, the gig public is driven by the will to visibility – a pursuit of attention, recognition and acknowledgement. These engagements not only privilege performative self-expression over critical, reasoned deliberation but also enable the commodification of communicative acts, attention and personal data. Rooted in the will to visibility and performative publicity, the gig public effectively performs generic labour for capital.

Despite its collaborative appearance, the habitual and contractual relationships that underpin the formation and expression of (public) opinion within the gig public distort the dynamics of public discourse. This undermines

Kant's vision of 'an entire public enlightening itself' through rational deliberation – a process that, according to him, requires only that the public be
'left in freedom':

> This is indeed almost inevitable, if only the public concerned is left in
> freedom. For there will always be a few who think for themselves, even
> among those appointed as guardians of the common mass. Such guard-
> ians, once they have themselves thrown off the yoke of immaturity, will
> disseminate the spirit of rational respect for personal value and for the
> duty of all men to think for themselves. (Kant 1784)

Yet, the gig public finds itself paradoxically constrained – ostensibly free but
lost in its freedom while shackled by the algorithmic 'yoke of immaturity',
enforced by the habitual and contractual practices imposed by surveillance
capitalism. While it possesses the potential to facilitate rapid information
exchange and amplify diverse voices, its dependence on profit-driven platforms weakens its emancipatory capacity. It devolves instead into a mechanism that perpetuates intellectual immaturity and passivity, governed by
economic imperatives and algorithmic nudges. The potential of the public for
critical reflection and collective enlightenment is compromised, as individuals are often guided not by autonomous reflection on the reliability of their
own and others' judgements but rather by the platforms' economic and algorithmic constraints on visibility.

These conditions inhibit the escape from self-incurred immaturity envisioned by Kant, replacing a commitment to critical and reasoned debate with
a commodified, algorithmically curated form of performative publicness. This
shift reflects deeper structural transformations in the relationship between
individuals, corporate media and the logics of surveillance capitalism. As a
result, the gig public is often – though not inevitably – instrumentalised in ways
that exacerbate epistemic segregation and political polarisation, while systematically undermining the possibilities for genuine deliberative engagement.

This *paradox of freedom* in the gig public can only be resolved through *structural* and *regulatory* interventions aimed at the technological, politico-economic
and cultural pillars of the public sphere's infrastructure. Additionally, a *cultural* shift is necessary to foster genuine autonomy and freedom of expression
while cultivating a reflexive and mediative quality in public discourse. The
final chapter will explore actionable pathways forward, reflecting on current
conditions and envisioning a more mature, deliberative public capable of sustaining democratic values in the digital age.

Chapter 4

INVIGORATING PUBLICNESS
IN THE AI WORLD

Challenges, Opportunities and Strategies

This concluding chapter explores the potential to revitalise publicness in the age of artificial intelligence. It focuses on how contemporary AI-based epistemic technologies, which amplify human knowledge-making capacities, reshape the relationship between access and rational-critical discourse. Rather than assuming that greater access necessarily strengthens publicness, the chapter interrogates this assumption, outlining strategies to resist fragmentation and foster democratic capacities in a digital world increasingly structured by algorithmic infrastructures.

Revolutionising Publicness: How Epistemic Technologies Shape Public Discourse

This section explores how epistemic technologies, which externalise and automate cognitive processes once performed exclusively by the human brain, have deeply transformed dynamics of public discourse. AI systems capable of producing human-like text, generating images and video and automating decisions reconfigure how knowledge is created, circulated and legitimised. These developments challenge classical conditions for public engagement by destabilising traditional authority structures and altering the pace and scale of communicative participation.

The Accessibility Paradox: Are AI Technologies Adapting Humans?

Drawing on Plato's philosophical concerns about writing as an externalisation of memory and McLuhan's prophetic insights into the technological simulation of consciousness, this section analyses the paradox that underpins today's digital communication landscape: Although epistemic technologies expand access to information and expression, they simultaneously personalise, filter and curate content in ways that undercut rational-critical discourse, amplify visibility and emotions, fragment publics and threaten the ideals of inclusive dialogue and collective deliberation.

Publics in the Algorithmic Age: Pathways to Democratic Empowerment

The final section turns to the possibilities for enhancing citizen engagement and cultivating meaningful participation in the public sphere. It addresses the multifaceted challenges posed by digital platforms, AI-driven systems and the surveillance economy, and outlines potential interventions – such as educational initiatives, participatory design and regulatory reforms – aimed at mitigating their disempowering effects. While the full realisation of publicness remains constrained by current socio-technical conditions, these strategies offer pathways for sustaining moments of democratic engagement and for resisting the alienation and disempowerment of citizens.

* * *

The age of artificial intelligence has profoundly transformed the nature of publicness and the public sphere by enabling diverse forms of communication via media platforms and technological systems – a transformation further amplified by the emergence of epistemic technologies such as generative AI. These advancements have catalysed significant changes in how the public sphere functions, starkly contrasting with its normative conceptualisations and exposing the tension between idealised frameworks and the complexities of real social relations.

Under these altered socio-technical conditions, reconceptualising the public sphere as an infrastructure of publicness challenges traditional assumptions that define it primarily as a space for rational deliberation, debate and, hopefully, consensus-building. While affirming publicness as central to democratic legitimacy, this approach – rooted in the critical sociological tradition that arose during the transition from the nineteenth to the twentieth century – reframes the public sphere as a dynamic and contested domain shaped by competing interests and persistent tensions. However, this democratically organised infrastructure – balancing inclusivity, pluralism and accountability, and essential to establishing conditions of collective will-formation – appears fundamentally compromised in the era of surveillance capitalism. While this perspective affirms the core principles of deliberative democracy, it also situates them within the broader material and cultural systems that shape and constrain deliberative practices.

Moving beyond idealised and prescriptive models, this empirically grounded approach identifies clear standards for democratic discourse – ensuring broad access, welcoming diverse voices and representing varied perspectives. As outlined in the introductory chapter, it offers practical tools to assess and strengthen the public sphere without imposing a singular, universalist model of public communication. It rejects narrow definitions of the public sphere based on bourgeois idealisations of rational discourse and instead embraces the diversity of communicative styles, interests and cultural contexts.

Moreover, it highlights how the technological, institutional and cultural foundations of publicness can either reproduce or challenge entrenched exclusions based on gender, class, race and other social inequalities. Acknowledging that public discourse is shaped by power dynamics and historical contingencies rather than abstract normative ideals, this perspective sees infrastructure not as a guarantee of publicness, but as a necessary – yet always contested – condition within which communicative power is continually negotiated.

In this context, the public sphere shifts from being a neutral infrastructure of publicness to a battleground where political, economic, governmental and civic actors compete for influence. Communication within this space is no longer autonomously self-regulated – if it ever truly was, beyond the claims of normative theory – but is increasingly orchestrated and governed by digital platforms. These platforms, functioning as a novel form of enterprise shaped by the profit-driven logic of the surveillance economy, prioritise the maximisation of content supply, accessibility and usage while capturing user attention and advertising revenue. This prioritisation ensures the platforms – not contributors – extract the greatest share of profit, fundamentally altering the dynamics of public communication.

This reconceptualisation of the public sphere builds on the core dimensions of publicness outlined in the *VARMIL* framework (Splichal 2022): visibility, access, reflexive publicity, mediation, influence and legitimisation. As introduced briefly in the introduction, these components underscore that meaningful public discourse depends not only on the content of ideas being exchanged but also on the socio-technical systems that enable or obstruct such exchanges.

At the heart of this transformation lies the emergence of the gig public – a new mode of public engagement shaped by three powerful forces: the digitisation and hyper-connectivity of social life, the epistemic power of AI and other knowledge-shaping technologies, and the commodification of attention and behaviour under surveillance capitalism.

The differences between the Enlightenment-inspired normative model of the reasoned public and the analytical model of the gig public can be productively examined through the six *VARMIL* components, which shape the distinct dynamics of public discourse within each paradigm:

	The Reasoned Public	*The Gig Public*
Visibility	Visibility serves as a mechanism for identifying, monitoring, and debating matters of public concern. It is tied to issue salience and deliberative relevance. Attention is earned through informed discussion aimed at collective outcomes, whether in policymaking, academic debates, or civic engagement.	Personal visibility is an end in itself. It is driven by algorithmic amplification and spectacle. Attention is captured through emotion, virality, and performative content, leading to a public space dominated by fleeting, surface-level interactions heavily influenced by trends and media spectacle.
Access	Formally open via rights and citizenship, but practically shaped by expertise, organisational affiliation or demonstrated credibility. While such gatekeeping can help maintain the quality of discourse, it also imposes barriers to broader and more inclusive participation.	Universally open, allowing virtually anyone to participate without vetting or credentialing. This inclusivity not only fosters broad participation and diverse perspectives but also exposes discourse to misinformation, manipulation and low-quality contributions.
Reflexivity	Civic autonomy is grounded in reason, responsibility and shared norms. Participants see themselves as contributors to democratic deliberation, critically assess their own arguments, engage thoughtfully with opposing viewpoints, adjust positions and pursue mutual understanding. Discursive practices build cognitive resilience, civic trust and capacity for judgement.	Reflexivity is substituted by performativity. Users act strategically within platform constraints. The self is curated for visibility, shaped by metrics and performative incentives. Engagement is reactive, emotionally affirming and driven by habitual and contractual dynamic. It reinforces preexisting beliefs within epistemic enclaves, limiting deep engagement or ethical challenge. Trends, hashtags and emotional triggers create the illusion of shared concern without sustained discourse.

(*Continued*)

(Continued)

The Reasoned Public	*The Gig Public*
Mediativity	Strong and institutionalised mediativity is structured by transparent interfaces between rulers and the ruled, institutional power and civil society, and among actors participating in the public sphere (journalism, academia, civil society). These structures validate, moderate and contextualise public discourse. Recognition of common concerns arises through mutual framing of shared consequences requiring collective response.	Weak mediativity is substituted by performativity, shaped by opaque platform governance and driven by engagement metrics that amplify polarising, emotionally charged and entertainment-oriented content. It lacks epistemic filtering or normative anchoring. Cognitive overload and attention fragmentation drain civic energy and reduce deliberative potential.
Influence	Influence is procedural and institutional, emerging from principles of rational deliberation and evidence-based argumentation. It derives persuasive power from collective engagement rooted in shared values, which informs 'solid' public opinion, shapes policy agendas and holds decision-makers accountable through discursive legitimisation.	Influence is reactive, episodic and viral, often decoupled from institutional channels and deliberative processes, and shaped by manipulative forces – including corporate agendas, political propaganda and the volatility of online popularity. Public opinion is 'gaseous': emotionally volatile, manipulable and prone to rapid dissipation.
Legitimisation	Legitimacy is conferred through critical evaluation of public claims, decisions or positions based on reasoned justification, evidence and procedural norms, thereby fostering public trust in democratic processes and institutions.	Legitimacy is based on visibility, popularity or emotional resonance. It is unstable and spectacle-driven. Authorities gain or lose legitimacy depending on their ability to attract attention and perform effectively within algorithmically governed media environments.

Digital platforms central to the rise of gig publics no longer serve as inter-mediaries mediating between those in power and the governed – as Marx once described the press – but have instead become profit-driven enter-prises whose objectives diverge sharply from the principles of publicness and communicative freedom. Their algorithmic systems prioritise content based on metrics of profitability and user engagement, often amplifying disinformation while sidelining core democratic values such as inclusivity, diversity and even truth. By privileging content that maximises profit over fostering public-worthy information and democratic deliberation, these platforms create a structural imbalance in the flow and quality of public communication. This imbalance systematically amplifies polarising or sensational content while relegating substantive discourse. Shared informational spaces are thereby eroded, leading to a fragmented and increasingly divided public sphere.

To avoid Dewey's bleak scenario of a fragmented publics – where too many isolated and disconnected publics emerge – it is crucial to develop a clear vision to guide efforts for invigorating publicness. In an era of generative AI, where technology-driven and capital-oriented innovations outpace the societal regulations that should ideally guide them, revitalising publicness calls for bold, forward-looking strategies. The decentralising potential of blockchain technologies, combined with the grassroots movements seeking to reclaim the Internet from global digital platform giants, offers a promising pathway towards reviving the civic potential of digital technologies – a foundation essential for (re)invigorating publicness.

At the core of this revitalisation is the need to confront the accessibility paradox: the simultaneous expansion of access to information and the growing fragmentation of publics caused by highly curated and extensively consumed personalised content. Epistemic technologies, while transformative, risk undermining the shared discursive spaces necessary for inclusive dialogue and collective deliberation.

Drawing on Murdock and Golding's (1989) foundational conception of communication rights – which includes maximising access to information about individual rights, ensuring that diverse communities have access to a range of information sources, and enabling all societal groups to be represented in media and to actively shape those representations – these rights must now be expanded to meet the demands of the AI era. New rights should include individuals' control over participation in AI-mediated communication; access to verified and public-worthy information and knowledge necessary for meaningful engagement; and the creation of – as well as access to – educational opportunities, which form the necessary foundation for exercising all other communication-related rights. These additions underscore the urgent need to empower citizens to participate effectively – and in solidarity – within an ever more complex, algorithmically mediated public sphere.

Revolutionising Publicness: How Epistemic Technologies Shape Public Discourse

To understand this transformation, we first examine how AI systems that automate cognitive processes have intensified the reconfiguration of the very foundations of public discourse initiated by earlier communication technologies. The evolution of such technologies has always been closely tied to their epistemic functions. Major technological breakthroughs have not only enhanced the quantitative aspects of communication – accelerating its speed, widening access and amplifying the volume of transmitted information – but have also significantly improved the qualitative capacities through which information is produced, verified, distributed and utilised. The evolution of public discourse has thus been shaped by the dynamic interplay between freedom of expression and the technologies that enable it. These technologies fulfil two critical epistemic roles: a historically foundational role in the dissemination of knowledge, and a creative, cognitive role in the generation of new knowledge.

The technology of printing was championed by Enlightenment thinkers as a technology of freedom, serving as a vehicle for materialising individual *freedom of the pen* (Kant) and for *expressing the common will* (Tönnies). It promoted reasoned discourse and helped cultivate an informed public. In the mid-1800s, Marx saw the press, in its ideal form, as a vital bond connecting citizens – acting also as an intermediary between those in power and the governed – with freedom of the press constituting a quintessential cornerstone of political emancipation. A half-century later, Gabriel Tarde highlighted the pivotal role of newspapers in creating *the public* – an emerging sociological category linked to the spread of print media – and shaping processes of public opinion. A few decades after Tarde, Bertolt Brecht reimagined radio not merely as a one-way broadcasting tool, but as a medium for interactive, two-way communication, capable of democratising discourse and empowering individuals.

This optimistic view of communication technologies has persisted throughout history, though it has often been contradicted by their practical misuse in support of counter-public epistemic aims. Consider the revolutionary impact of printing on free expression: While this technology initially challenged representative forms of publicness rooted in status and authority, the expansion of the press to broader audiences also facilitated a shift from individual freedom of expression to corporate freedom of the press – a form of entrepreneurial liberty that enables powerful entities to shape public opinion.

This pattern has repeated with each new wave of communication technology. Time and again, dominant political and economic actors have curtailed the democratic potential of these technologies by harnessing them for ideological manipulation, instrumental publicity and representative publicness. This recurring dynamic produces twin outcomes: growing concentration of power among elites, alongside the rise of increasingly sophisticated forms of technical slavery.

The advent of digital technology and the Internet ushered in a new form of publicness, anchoring freedom in the will to visibility. This transformation gave rise to performative publicness, where individuals and organisations strategically curate their self-presentation within a space under perpetual digital surveillance. What was once envisioned as a domain for reasoned debate and critique has, in many cases, become a stage for visibility management and monetisation, transmuting traditional representative publicness into a more adaptive, algorithmically mediated and performance-driven form. Generative AI has dramatically amplified these tensions, compelling us to confront the profound and long-term societal consequences of communication technologies as they reshape human experience and cognition across every domain of creativity – from science and education to the arts and media.

The evolution of communication technologies signals a fundamental transformation in how we engage with knowledge: We have progressed from technologies that extend our senses to those that extend our cognition. Traditional communication technologies – from spoken language and writing to printing presses, radio and television – served as what McLuhan (1964) termed 'extensions of our senses', enhancing visual, auditory and tactile perception. These innovations amplified sensory experience, enabled long-distance communication and profoundly reshaped human perception, social interaction and societal organisation. Yet crucially, they all required human interpretation and cognitive processing to interpret and give meaning to sensory data.

AI-based communication technologies represent a quantum leap – they now function as extensions of human cognition itself. This shift from sensory to cognitive augmentation marks a pivotal moment in technological history. Whereas previous technologies primarily extended our sensory capacities – expanding what we could perceive (enhancing observation and communication) – AI-based systems augment our cognitive faculties, fundamentally altering how we produce, process and exchange knowledge. These systems increasingly perform core cognitive functions: synthesising complex information, conducting autonomous analysis and generating original content. In doing so, they are fundamentally restructuring the epistemic underpinnings of public discourse.

This transformation also calls into question our traditional understanding of epistemic technologies. Historically, such technologies were conceived as primarily cognitive tools – such as books, libraries or teaching methods – that existed within the social domain. A classical distinction separated physical technologies (like machinery or physical infrastructure) from the cognitive, knowledge-oriented functions of social technologies. For instance, the printing press was seen as a material device, while the book was understood as a social/epistemic artifact – a tool for the dissemination and preservation of knowledge within a social context.

However, by enabling mass production of newspapers and literature, printing technology also assumed profound epistemic consequences – democratising access to knowledge, challenging established power dynamics and catalysing societal transformation. These two modes of technological operation – altering or manipulating physical matter and influencing human thought, perception or behaviour – are now inseparably intertwined in contemporary AI systems. For example, AI – in the form of chatbots, recommendation algorithms or virtual assistants – does not merely respond to user queries in a mechanical sense; it actively shapes the inquiry process itself by framing what information is presented, prioritised or omitted. This expands our conception of epistemic technologies beyond abstract cognitive tools to include integrated systems that combine both material and cognitive processes – systems with the capacity not only to enhance but potentially to replace human intelligence and agency.

Over sixty years ago, Marshall McLuhan anticipated this development in his vision of the 'final phase' of technological evolution. He argued that, following the extension of the human body through mechanical technologies and the central nervous system through electric media, society was approaching the extension of consciousness itself:

> Rapidly, we approach the final phase of the extensions of man – the *technological simulation of consciousness*, when the creative process of knowing will be collectively and corporately extended to the whole of human society, much as we have already extended our senses and our nerves by the various media. Whether the *extension of consciousness*, so long sought by advertisers for specific products, will be 'a good thing' is a question that admits of a wide solution. (McLuhan 1964/1994, 3; emphasis added)

This prophetic insight resonates powerfully today. Whereas traditional technologies allowed users to direct focus and interpret meaning, AI technologies, with their adaptive algorithms and predictive capacities, guide user attention, shape inquiry paths and influence decision-making in real time. Traditional media primarily served as conduits for disseminating pre-existing knowledge, largely shaped by human input. In contrast, AI technologies not only distribute knowledge but generate it – creating new content, identifying novel patterns,and extracting insights from massive datasets. This evolution fundamentally shifts the cognitive load: Users are no longer simply interpreting or retrieving information but are increasingly reliant on AI systems to manage, structure and even originate knowledge. As AI systems assume greater epistemic authority, the conditions under which knowledge is formed, shared and contested are being profoundly redefined.

AI-based communication technologies now play a far more decisive role in shaping the public sphere and publicness than any previous epistemic tool. They redefine the conditions of visibility, interactivity and influence, and reconfigure the very boundaries of publicness. What makes AI uniquely transformative is its scalability, adaptability, interactivity, capacity for real-time learning and data-driven insights. These features position AI as the most transformative epistemic technology in history, altering how knowledge is generated, verified, disseminated and appropriated.

Whereas earlier epistemic technologies were limited in reach and largely mediated by institutional structures or cultural norms – with knowledge production and dissemination often confined to academic or professional gatekeepers – AI-based communication technologies have dramatically expanded their societal impact. They have democratised knowledge and information, enhancing educational and creative experiences by enabling individuals to access vast knowledge repositories and create content that once required specialised training.

However, these advances also introduce serious challenges. The same technologies that democratise knowledge can facilitate the spread of misinformation, reinforce biases, raise intellectual property concerns and generate novel ethical dilemmas. The sheer volume of low-quality or misleading content risks eclipsing the work of qualified experts, thereby devaluing expertise and eroding public trust in knowledge institutions.

On one hand, AI has expanded participation in the production and circulation of knowledge. It has fostered collaborative knowledge work, enabled new forms of socialisation around information, restructured information flows and allowed for unprecedented interactivity. On the other hand, its deployment within commercially driven platforms has amplified misinformation and disinformation, weakening the coherence, inclusivity and rational-critical quality of public discourse. This duality reveals the complexity of the current media environment, in which gig publics must navigate the blurred line between credible information and manipulation.

This destabilisation of public discourse is acutely evident in the proliferation of disinformation campaigns, automated propaganda and political manipulation. AI-generated synthetic content increasingly obscures the boundary between fact and fiction, corroding trust in media and knowledge systems. The opaque, 'black box' nature of many AI systems complicates the task of verification, making it more difficult to distinguish between human- and machine-generated content.

AI chatbots, such as OpenAI's ChatGPT, have gained wide popularity for their versatility in performing personal and professional tasks, such as writing code, composing emails, drafting reports, generating art, writing Excel formulas and much more. However, despite significant efforts to embed safeguards, these systems can still be manipulated to bypass protections. This vulnerability allows malicious actors to exploit AI for disinformation campaigns, as illustrated by the emergence of AI-generated content on social media, often followed by automated responses from fake accounts controlled by similar systems (Nimmo 2024). This underscores the growing potential for AI-driven manipulation of public discourse, placing the foundations of informed public deliberation at serious risk and highlighting the need for stronger protections and oversight in digital environments.

AI has also fundamentally altered the relationship between content producers and users, reshaping the quality and inclusivity of public discourse. Media organisations increasingly deploy AI to track audience behaviour and preferences, dynamically adjusting content in real-time and making news consumption a more interactive experience. However, hyper-personalised storytelling and algorithmic recommendation systems also create epistemic enclaves, privileging emotional intensity or sensationalism over substantive deliberation and reinforcing polarisation. These dynamics not only undermine journalistic integrity but also erode shared understanding, thereby compromising the democratic function of the public sphere.

Beyond content curation, AI has fundamentally disrupted the economic foundations of media and journalism. Social media platforms and search engines, powered by AI algorithms, now dominate news distribution, disintermediating traditional media outlets and weakening both editorial accountability and the epistemic authority of journalism. Generative AI exacerbates these disruptions by introducing new modes of content production that threaten established news workflows. While AI presents new revenue opportunities, such as personalised subscriptions and targeted advertising, it also deepens reliance on data-driven business models. This shift centralises control in the hands of platform owners, reducing the independence of news organisations. Moreover, automation, while lowering operational costs, risks deskilling the journalism profession by concentrating editorial and technical expertise within a few powerful and well-resourced actors. Over time, this trend may reduce the diversity and quality of news production, threatening the epistemic pluralism essential to a vibrant and democratic public sphere.

Overall, the effects of AI-based epistemic technologies ripple through public deliberation in three significant ways. First, they undermine sustained reflection, as the immediacy and overwhelming volume of content on digital platforms leave little room for thoughtful analysis or extended deliberation. Second, they fragment publics and the public sphere, as personalisation algorithms isolate individuals into segregated 'micro-publics', making it increasingly difficult to cultivate collective understanding or establish a shared basis for democratic decision-making. Third, the opacity of algorithmic systems and the rise of disinformation erode public trust in both communication platforms and traditional journalism.

The deployment of AI-based epistemic technologies raises pressing ethical and democratic concerns about the future of public communication. How can media organisations – once 'organs of public opinion' – maintain editorial accountability, accuracy and fairness in an environment where opaque and externally governed AI systems increasingly shape the flow of information? While AI tools can assist in combating disinformation – through automated fact-checking and the detection of fake content – they may also contribute to further fragmentation of the public sphere, undermining journalism's deliberative function and prioritising viral engagement over issues of genuine public interest. Moreover, although AI holds the potential to amplify under-represented voices and diversify storytelling, poor governance and design choices risk reinforcing existing inequalities rather than resolving them.

These challenges to the quality and legitimacy of public discourse reveal the dual nature of AI-based epistemic transformations: They offer unprecedented opportunities for democratic participation while also posing serious barriers to achieving coherent and inclusive publicness in the AI age. That these dilemmas are not entirely new – given longstanding concerns in Western thought about the impact of cognitive and epistemic technologies on individuals and society – is perhaps cold comfort in our current predicament.

Plato, for instance, famously expressed scepticism about the effects of writing on human cognition and social interaction. In *Phaedrus*, Socrates critiques writing as an inferior mode of communication compared to speech, warning that it would diminish memory and undermine wisdom. Addressing Phaedrus, he says:

> This discovery of yours will create forgetfulness in the learners' souls, because they will not use their memories; they will trust to the external written characters and not remember of themselves. The specific which

you have discovered is an aid not to memory, but to reminiscence, and you give your disciples not truth, but only the semblance of truth; they will be hearers of many things and will have learned nothing; they will appear to be omniscient and will generally know nothing; they will be tiresome company, having the show of wisdom without the reality. (Plato 360 B.C.E.)

Plato's critique resonates powerfully with contemporary anxieties about generative AI. Both writing and GenAI are revolutionary epistemic technologies that profoundly reshape how knowledge is produced, stored and disseminated. Yet while Plato feared the passive consumption of externally stored knowledge, the challenges posed by GenAI are far more complex and destabilising. GenAI generates content at unprecedented speeds and scale, often without human oversight, complicating verification, authenticity and even the very definition of knowledge itself.

   Just as Plato warned that writing would erode memory, GenAI threatens to diminish critical thinking, as users increasingly outsource intellectual labour to machines. While writing expanded access to knowledge and helped democratise literacy, GenAI goes further by enabling nearly anyone to generate content. This democratisation, however, comes with the risk of an oversaturation of low-quality information, diminishing the value of expert insight, diluting the visibility of expert insight and crowding out epistemic nuance. Moreover, just as writing transformed dialogue into a one-way form of communication, GenAI may further isolate users within epistemic enclaves, where algorithmically tailored content reinforces pre-existing beliefs, thereby exacerbating societal divisions and undermining the possibility of shared, collective discourse.

   If Plato feared that writing would jeopardise memory, GenAI threatens something more radical: the displacement of human synthesis and judgement. This shift from static knowledge storage to dynamic, unverified creation marks what Jacques Ellul called the inversion of the relationship between civilisation and technique. While writing initiated a historical trajectory in which 'technique *belonged* to a civilization and was merely a single element among a host of nontechnical activities', Ellul warned that in the twentieth century this relationship had reversed:

> Today *technique has taken over the whole of civilization*. Certainly, technique is no longer the simple machine substitute for human labour. It has come to be the 'intervention into the very substance not only of the inorganic but also of the organic' (Ellul 1954/1964, 128).

For Ellul, technique had ceased to exist merely as a machine substitute for human labour and instead subordinated humans to its own logic. Both work and leisure, he argued, became mechanised and exploited by invasive techniques, submitting humans 'irreparably to technical slavery', leaving no true freedom of choice (ibid., 84).

While Plato may have overstated the dangers of externalised knowledge by writing, the advent of GenAI constitutes a more radical inversion: Technological systems now shape human behaviour, social norms and public discourse in real time. They do not merely store or transmit information; they generate, prioritise and circulate it algorithmically, often based on commercial or opaque criteria. This shift marks a departure from technologies that extended human capacities towards systems that actively intervene in human reasoning. This development raises more complex and urgent questions than those Plato could have anticipated – but which Ellul clearly foresaw. Whereas writing encouraged deliberation and careful articulation, GenAI collapses production and dissemination into instantaneous, personalised outputs – accelerating communication and amplifying diverse voices, but also disrupting shared meaning-making and fragmenting the public sphere into micro-publics.

The scale, speed and generativity of AI thus present epistemological and ethical dilemmas that far exceed the risks Plato associated with writing. These transformations demand a rethinking of how we engage with knowledge – and what it means to be wise in an AI-mediated world. They also call attention to the deeper challenge articulated nearly a century ago by John Dewey (1927/1954, 146): the problem of 'discovering the means by which a scattered, mobile, and manifold public may so recognize itself as to define and express its interests'. In the age of GenAI, this challenge is more pressing than ever.

The Accessibility Paradox: Are AI Technologies Adapting Humans?

The concept of the public has long been grounded in the principles of equal access and the fair representation of all voices in collective deliberation. The ideal of publicness is intrinsically tied to universal accessibility, aiming to ensure that citizens can freely access and meaningfully engage in shared processes of communication and understanding. Since the Enlightenment, media and journalism have played a central role in the historical effort to realise this ideal. The invention of the printing press supported these ambitions by expanding access to news, critique and a diversity of perspectives. For much of modern history, print media and journalism functioned as intermediaries between power and the citizenry, shaping public understanding and deliberation through editorial standards, professional integrity and institutional accountability.

Yet despite these advancements, efforts to realise the ideal of reflexive publicity – defined by informed debate, critique and accountability – have consistently fallen short. Marginalised voices have long struggled for equal representation in public discourse, underscoring the enduring challenges of achieving genuine publicness. Although new communication technologies have historically expanded visibility and access, they have often failed to foster meaningful engagement and, at times, have undermined the rational-critical character of public discourse.

This conundrum is evident in the rise of manipulative publicity and the declining legitimacy of public opinion, both of which are closely linked to technological developments. A central paradox of publicness lies in the tension between openness and deliberative quality: While openness is essential to reasoned debate, the expansion of the public sphere has often correlated with a decline in its rational-critical quality and a growing dominance of the will to visibility. As Habermas observed: 'Publicness seems to lose the power of its principle, critical publicity, to the extent that it expands as a sphere and still undermines the private realm' (1962/1990, 224; my translation, original emphasis).

Ellul (1964) identified the structural roots of this paradox in his commentary on Lewis Mumford's *Technics and Civilization* (1934), where Mumford contrasted the majestic, intricate nature of printing technology with the often vulgar and simplistic content of newspapers – content that, he argued, reflected limited, subjective and predominantly negative human emotions like hatred and fear. While Mumford did not link this content to the societal structure shaped by printing technology itself, Ellul contended that such content was neither incidental nor merely an 'abuse of technology'.Rather, he argued, it stemmed from the deliberate psychological and psychoanalytic techniques aimed at adapting individuals to the demands and conditions of technological society:

> This content is not the product of chance or of some economic form. It is the result of precise psychological and psychoanalytical techniques. These techniques have as their goal the bringing to the individual of that which is indispensable for his satisfaction in the conditions in which the machine has placed him, of inhibiting in him the sense of revolution, of subjugating him by flattering him. In other words, journalistic content is a technical complex expressly intended to adapt the man to the machine. (Ellul 1954/1964, 95)

Ellul's critique deepens earlier concerns raised by late nineteenth- and early twentieth-century thinkers who explored the contradictions inherent in the print media of early modern society. They examined the tension between

expanded access to the public sphere and the erosion of rationality in public discourse, as well as the persistent fragmentation of publics. Ferdinand
Tönnies (1922, 229), for instance, observed that the relationship between
access and rationality reflects broader social divisions, such as those between
capital and labour, urban and rural populations and the educated and unedu-
cated classes. He argued that the inclusion of historically marginalised voices
– women, rural citizens and the working class – posed a threat to the homogeneity and unity of public opinion, thereby revealing the inherent fragility of
a singular, reasoned public.

The Around the same time in the United States, the polemic between John
Dewey and Walter Lippmann highlighted the centrality of informed citizen engagement for democracy and the obstacles to achieving it. Lippmann
voiced scepticism about the public's capacity to form sound judgements in a
complex society, arguing that most citizens lack the time, information and
cognitive tools to meaningfully engage with public affairs. Dewey, by contrast, similarly to his contemporaries Tarde and Tönnies, argued that citizens
could navigate societal complexities if adequately supported by education and
access to reliable, scientific knowledge. For Dewey and his contemporaries,
raising educational standards and cultivating general knowledge – rooted in
the democratic promise of scientific progress – was essential to fostering an
informed and participatory public.

If Plato's critique of cognitive/epistemic technologies – voiced in his warning about the dangers of writing – once seemed exaggerated, it now appears
remarkably prescient in the age of generative AI. While writing externalised
memory and transformed knowledge transmission without fundamentally
compromising human critical faculties, GenAI poses far deeper challenges.
It externalises core cognitive functions like synthesis and analysis, while
simultaneously eroding critical thinking, amplifying misinformation and
fragmenting public discourse on an unprecedented scale. Plato's fear that the
mere semblance of wisdom might replace genuine understanding finds a dis-
quieting echo in the dynamics of GenAI.

The AI-driven transformation of publicness – arguably the most significant communicative shift in modern history – has intensified the accessibility
paradox more than any previous technological innovation. Individuals now
enjoy unparalleled opportunities to express and share their viewpoints, yet
this has come at the cost of the quality of public discourse. The rise of digitalisation, combined with the entrepreneurial logic of online platforms, has
fragmented public-worthy debates into vast, polarised domains embedded
within integrated public–private communication networks.

This development highlights the core of the accessibility paradox, exposing a critical distinction between mere access and meaningful involvement.

While digital technologies, amplified by artificial intelligence, have broadened access to communication channels and increased the visibility of social issues, they have also intensified the drive for visibility and the performative nature of publicness. Individuals increasingly curate their online presence to project idealised selves, a trend that undermines the rational-critical engagement essential for the formation of authentic publics. As a result, deliberation is curtailed by performance and participation is reduced to acts of impression management.

While AI was initially heralded as a tool that could elevate rationality – by synthesising information, reducing bias and fostering evidence-based debate – its deployment on social media platforms has often had the opposite effect. GenAI-driven recommendation systems optimise content for engagement in ways that amplify emotional contagion. Rather than fostering logical persuasion and dialectical progress towards truth, these systems reinforce users' preexisting opinions and beliefs. As a result, content that triggers strong emotional responses – such as outrage, fear or enthusiasm – tends to spread faster than measured, rational discourse. This dynamic recalls the ancient Greek contrast between *logos* (reasoned argument) and *pathos* (emotional appeal), as well as between *doxa* (opinion) and *episteme* (knowledge) – with contemporary platforms systematically privileging opinion and emotion by design.

Tönnies recognised this tension in public opinion, noting that 'emotion is especially characteristic of the great multitude' constituting publics, while 'the leaders are naturally distinguished by superior consciousness [...] and, as intellectuals, are more practiced in thinking, as is generally the older man and the master of every art, every craft' (Tönnies 1922, 206). He observed the contradiction between the theoretical conceptualisation of public opinion and its empirical, 'fluid' manifestation: 'Public opinion seldom aligns with the idealised concept of public opinion as the mental form of the rational social will (*Kürwille*). Yet, it perceives the affect that dominates it as something foreign while asserting a claim to truth and validity' (ibid., 249).

The rise of AI-driven epistemic technologies represents a fundamental shift in how communication tools shape the nature and scope of public discourse. Unlike earlier technologies that applied existing information in practical contexts and broadcast pre-curated content to mass audiences, the new generation of AI-driven systems autonomously curates and generates content, shaping knowledge production and influencing decision-making processes. This 'reverse flow' of content – from editorially guided institutions (such as newsrooms) to algorithmically driven platforms (like YouTube and Facebook) – reconfigures visibility and newsworthiness: Rather than being selected based on editorial judgement, content is now filtered and ranked according to inferred user preferences, engagement metrics and platform profit motives.

Whereas content was previously curated by human editors and disseminated top-down to audiences, it is now increasingly generated and modu-
lated bottom-up by algorithmic systems that 'respond' in real time to users'
calculated habits and preferences. As a result, traditional journalism – long
regarded as an organ of public opinion – now finds itself in direct competition
with social media platforms for audience attention.

The proliferation of the printed word historically enabled a clear distinction 'between information (or knowledge), on the one side, and on the other,
the attitudes and sentiments – the affect structure – to which that information
is related' (Gouldner 1976, 105). This separation was believed to maintain
rational public discourse relatively insulated from the affective immediacy
inherent in face-to-face communication. By contrast, contemporary social
media has reintroduced affect as a central component of public communication, blurring not only the boundary between private and public discourse
but also the distinctions between fact and value, data and policy, and information and ideology – distinctions that, even historically, may never have
been as clear-cut as presumed.

To move beyond lamenting this erosion of boundaries, we can turn to
Weber's (1921/2019) distinction between instrumental and value rationality.
Instrumental rationality is oriented towards achieving efficient outcomes,
whereas value rationality pursues ends considered inherently legitimate or
morally right. This framework clarifies that rationality is not devoid of emotion: Value-rational actions often carry strong affective dimensions, rooted
in deeply held beliefs and commitments. As Tönnies observed, 'emotional
politics [is] the playground of public opinion', and public sentiment 'can often
coincide wonderfully with a planned rational politics' (Tönnies 1922, 253).
For him, individuals' ideas were expressions of both feeling and conscious
volition, directed towards specific ends and means. Thus, he insisted on the
need to 'return to common feelings and common wills in order to explain – at
least to a certain extent – common opinions' (ibid., 44).

Rather than framing emotion and affect as antithetical to rationality in
public discourse – treating them as if they stand in antagonistic opposition –
it is more productive to understand discourse and affect as interdependent.
Discourse does not merely tame or codify affect; as thinkers like Weber and
Tönnies suggest, affect plays a constitutive role in public deliberation and
decision-making. This insight is especially crucial in the context of algorithmically mediated public discourse, where affective dimensions become more
visible, amplified and intensified – even though they have always operated,
albeit more subtly, beneath the surface.

Traditional models of public discourse, particularly in the print era, often
idealised a strict separation between affect and rational deliberation, casting

affect as automatic, involuntary and idiosyncratic, in contrast to the conscious, planned and deliberative nature of rational argument. Yet this division was likely more aspirational than actual. The approaches of Weber and Tönnies help us recognise that affect and rationality not only coexist but are mutually constitutive: *Instrumental rationality*, focused on efficient means, may appear more detached and utilitarian, whereas *value rationality* is grounded in emotionally charged commitments and ethical convictions.

If we address the question of how the public is formed, the issue is not how affect and discourse relate in the abstract, but how they coalesce in discursive-affective networks that emerge, cluster and dissolve in everyday life – and with what social consequences. Within these networks, affect may be at times dominant, at other times peripheral, but it is never absent; it shapes who gets to speak, what is said and how it is received.

This dynamic becomes starkly visible in the platform-mediated public sphere, where the interplay of affect and discourse is actively engineered through algorithmic curation. Engagement-focused platforms incentivise emotionally charged, polarising and sensational content – rewarding what captures attention, not what deepens understanding. As professional journalism competes with viral content under the platform-imposed rules of supply and demand, the very conditions for forming a reflexive, dialogic public are undermined. Viral, bite-sized content increasingly overshadows quality investigative journalism, weakening professional principles, editorial standards and journalism's capacity to foster informed, reasoned publics.

What emerges instead are fragmented *gig publics* – temporary, reactive groupings organised around affective resonance rather than shared deliberation. These publics often cohere not through sustained reasoning, but through emotional contagion, performative alignment and algorithmic visibility. Even when participants diverge ideologically, they may remain tethered through shared emotional tone or reaction, forming enclaves that feel cohesive yet remain epistemically isolated. These enclaves are largely driven, neutralised or entrapped by affect – homogenised through shared emotional expression and public displays of sentiment, despite or beyond ideological differences (Papacharissi 2015, 7).

In this context, the question of how the public is formed must attend not only to discourse but also to the intensifying affective, AI-driven infrastructures that shape visibility, amplify resonance and affect the conditions for collective reasoning. As a result, the very concept of the public needs to be redefined: *Gig publics* shift the focus from shared understanding to reactive engagement, fragmenting into isolated epistemic enclaves and revealing both the emotional benefits and costs they may entail.

At the heart of these transformations lies the accessibility paradox of publicness. Digital platforms, armed with epistemic technologies, have democratised access to information and broadened participation in public discourse. Yet this democratisation carries a significant drawback: It often manipulates users who lack the education or critical tools to engage meaningfully with complex social issues. Spaces for public dialogue increasingly blend personal interactions with broader debates, creating environments that are highly accessible yet inherently chaotic. While this convergence can foster new forms of political engagement – making discourse more personal and approachable – it also risks diluting the clarity and coherence necessary for deliberation. As emotional content often dominates, the rational-critical principles essential for informed debate begin to erode, weakening society's capacity for collective accountability.

The democratisation of communication enabled by digital platforms can inadvertently perpetuate existing inequalities – a recurring theme in media history. Historically, the emergence of sensationalist media has correlated with declining rational discourse, a trend repeating itself in the transition from print to digital. While traditional media have long struggled to reach audiences, the rise of social media introduces new barriers to coherent public deliberation. These historical parallels underscore the need for deliberate efforts to address the challenges posed by increased access and visibility, particularly by strengthening citizens' capacities for critical engagement in an era of information overload.

The expanded access to communication networks and the resulting forms of publicness reveal a fundamental paradox at the heart of digitisation and communification. It exemplifies the enduring tension between technological empowerment and the concentration of power – a dynamic traceable back to the invention of writing. While digital communication has achieved near-universal global reach, it has weakened rather than strengthened reflexive publicity, instead promoting representative and performative forms of public engagement. This development fundamentally challenges the authenticity and legitimacy of digitally constituted publicness, as genuine publicness requires not just access but meaningful universal participation.

The contradiction between increased access and declining communication rationality has always existed. However, as long as market-regulated access to media remained open to competition and growth – despite constraints imposed by technological affordances and financial limitations, as in the case of the press and broadcasting – the commodifying effects of market logic were often considered politically acceptable. The early phases of digital communication promised to overcome the previous limitations of mass media, expanding the democratic potential of communication by transcending spatial and temporal boundaries and making communicative and educational resources more broadly accessible. The mass production of affordable mobile devices brought online participation within reach of much of the global population, ushering in an era of unprecedented connectivity.

Current developments, however, mark a decisive break from these earlier patterns. AI-driven epistemic technologies are now concentrated within an oligopoly of platform corporations, effectively precluding competition and alternative development models. This concentration revives important sociological insights often marginalised by dominant public sphere theories: namely, that publics transcend mere 'social categories' – large social groups sharing attributes without necessarily interaction. This long-standing concern, present since the late nineteenth century, draws attention to the complex interplay between social context and the socio-technical mechanisms that shape public discourse.

The accessibility paradox ultimately reveals that connectivity alone cannot ensure democratic engagement. It calls for a dual response: First, the deliberate and democratically accountable governance of the design and development of the socio-technical infrastructures that mediate publicness; and second, the cultivation of intellectual and civic capacities essential for upholding democratic norms, fostering inclusive publics and sustaining meaningful public discourse.

Publics in the Algorithmic Age: Pathways to Democratic Empowerment

To actualise Kant's vision of enlightenment, the gig public must transcend the constraints of surveillance capitalism, which requires a fundamental reimagining of platform governance. This shift demands moving regulatory principles away from profit-driven imperatives towards a framework balancing openness with critical, in-depth and sustained engagement. This entails addressing socio-technical and structural barriers: the monopolistic control of digital platforms, the algorithmic biases and inequalities they (re)produce and the commodification of user interactions.

These reforms are essential for unlocking the gig public's potential to foster meaningful discourse and enable collective democratic action. A crucial step in this involves socialising recommendation algorithms, redirecting their purpose from profit maximisation – based on the commodification of user attention and behaviour via surveillance, behavioural manipulation and standardisation – towards enhancing the public-worthiness of the content they recommend. As mediators between customs/traditions and contracts/conventions, algorithms play a critical role in shaping both individual opinion formation and the broader dynamics of public opinion. Their design determines whether they entrench opinion enclaves or foster inclusive, high-quality discourse.

The path algorithms take depends fundamentally on their design parameters, which reflect underlying economic and political priorities. Those prioritising homogeneity and bias reinforcement exacerbate fragmentation and polarisation, undermining democratic deliberation. Conversely, thoughtfully crafted algorithms can mitigate these risks by summarising complex information in accessible formats, encouraging critical engagement, promoting cognitive diversity and facilitating constructive, self-reflexive discourse.

Substantive structural and institutional reforms are necessary to advance equitable governance – ensuring fairness, inclusivity and justice in how power, resources and decision-making are distributed, particularly in contexts where technology mediates public life. Current legal frameworks, which should counter algorithmic biases, corporate dominance and systemic inequalities while ensuring public-interest accountability, remain woefully inadequate against rapid technological advancement.

Legislative intervention is critical to socialise algorithms, redirecting them from profit-driven management of habitual and contractual behaviour in gig publics towards fostering reflexivity, mediativity and public-worthiness of discourse. Equitable governance must address how AI-driven behaviours affect the performativisation of publicness. While habitual relationships (e.g., shared customs) can foster a sense of community and mutual understanding, they often suppress critical debate in complex societies. Conversely, contractual systems (e.g., platform rules) provide structure but, without sufficient user agency, reinforce exclusivity and hierarchical dynamics. The challenge lies in balancing these dynamics to prevent gig publics from being wholly shaped by market forces.

Meaningful change requires active involvement of *the state* and its *legislative power* –Tönnies' third complex form of social will interacting with public opinion. Legislative action is indispensable to counter the erosion of publicness caused by pervasive AI-driven communification and corporate capture of digital communication infrastructures. Yet complications arise as states themselves increasingly deploy generative AI and algorithmic tools, creating inherent conflicts of interest in regulating technologies they also rely upon.

These tensions call for rigorous scrutiny of AI applications not only in communication networks that host public discourse but also across domains such as education, policing and legislation itself – where algorithmic decision-making risks reinforcing systemic injustices, including economic marginalisation and racial inequality. Addressing these risks demands that policymakers deepen their understanding of technological infrastructures and their societal ramifications. This requires sustained collaboration with technologists, civil society actors and independent oversight bodies to ensure transparency, accountability and ethical governance.

Crucially, reactive regulation – intervening only after technologies are deployed – cannot achieve radical reform. Once embedded in socio-technical systems, the negative consequences of AI systems often become entrenched and difficult to reverse. Given the profound influence of algorithmic infrastructures on public discourse, their design must not be driven solely by technical efficiency, market imperatives or post hoc regulatory compliance. Ethical and social considerations must be embedded at the design stage, when their trajectory can still be shaped and potential harms mitigated.

Approaches such as Value Sensitive Design (Friedman and Hendry 2019) offer a concrete framework for ethical technological development by systematically integrating fundamental values like freedom, justice, autonomy, privacy and both individual and societal well-being. This methodology explicitly rejects the notion of technological neutrality, insisting that human values must guide innovation alongside functionality and economic feasibility. It employs an interdisciplinary, iterative approach comprising three integrated analytical dimensions. First, conceptual analysis identifies and defines stakeholder values through ethical theory and critical technology assessment. Second, empirical analysis applies social science research methods – such as interviews, surveys and observation – to examine user perspectives and community needs. Third, technical analysis evaluates how design choices affect value realisation and assesses the technological capacity to support ethical goals. These parallel, iterative processes work together to ensure values permeate the entire design lifecycle.

VSD and similar approaches are applicable across key technological developments, from privacy-protecting digital platforms and bias-mitigating AI decision systems to equitable smart city infrastructures. The approach is particularly vital for public discourse algorithms, offering an alternative to profit-driven designs by embedding core values of transparency, fairness and inclusivity. Such frameworks can help counteract epistemic enclaves while fostering critical engagement with diverse perspectives.

To support the regulation of technological developments, several interventions can enhance digital transparency and empower users – enabling greater control over their AI-mediated experiences in domains where they often lack adequate information, tools and critical awareness. Algorithmic literacy programmes should educate users about data collection practices, usage patterns and the broader impacts of AI systems. Governance transparency measures must disclose recommendation logic, explain content prioritisation and provide mechanisms for user adjustment. Additionally, public-worthiness algorithms, developed through collaborative and participatory processes, could prioritise socially significant content, support diverse viewpoints and promote collective well-being. This comprehensive approach aligns with Dewey's concept of publics as emergent formations constituted in response to the significant consequences of social actions and the need for regulatory intervention – precisely the dynamic shaped by modern algorithmic systems that mediate public discourse, economic transactions and social relations.

The challenge of algorithmic opacity presents a significant barrier to democratic discourse. Unlike traditional media, where audiences could assess and compare editorial policies, journalistic standards and ideological leanings across different outlets, algorithmic curation operates through concealed selection criteria, obscures content suppression mechanisms and prevents meaningful comparative analysis. This structural opacity systematically erodes foundational democratic principles, including transparency in decision-making, accountability for systemic impacts and reflexivity in public reasoning.

To counter these tendencies and revitalise democratic deliberation, coordinated strategies must move beyond individualistic and purely technical solutions. The necessary changes must be undertaken as a collective endeavour aimed at configuring a fundamentally different form of publicness – one that reaffirms Enlightenment ideals of publicness and transcends the narrow vision of performative, profit- and data-driven publicness presented by digital oligarchs as user-friendly inevitabilities. This transformation demands both immediate interventions and a long-term societal commitment to building the normative, institutional and infrastructural foundations necessary for value-centred technological development that prioritises democratic principles over commercial interests.

User Empowerment through Improved Algorithmic Transparency. Online public spaces must be designed to facilitate structured debate and reflexive participation. Moderation techniques that promote respectful and reasoned exchange can help cultivate environments where complex issues are explored without resorting to emotional or hostile reactions. Yet such environments require more than just effective moderation; they also demand greater user understanding of – and control over – the algorithmic systems that shape what is seen, shared and prioritised.

At present, however, most algorithmic systems are optimised primarily for user engagement rather than supporting informed, meaningful public discourse. Most available tools only reveal who collects users' data – not who it is shared with or for what purposes. This is a serious limitation in today's digital landscape, largely due to the opacity of data broker networks and platform privacy policies. Browser extensions like *Ghostery*, *Privacy Badger* and *uBlock*

Origin can reveal who is collecting user data (e.g., Google Analytics, Facebook Pixel) and what types of data are being transmitted (e.g., cookies, device fingerprinting, location). However, users cannot see what happens to their data after collection – for instance, who it is sold or shared with downstream (e.g., data brokers, advertisers, governments), what inferences are drawn (e.g., political views, income level, health status) or how these inferences are used (e.g., to shape personalised news feeds, credit scoring or micro-targeted advertising). This opacity highlights the need for stronger mechanisms of algorithmic accountability.

To close this gap, users of algorithm-driven services must be granted access to detailed information about the entire lifecycle of their data. This includes understanding whose interests are served by the extraction, storage and manipulation of their personal information, as well as how *user personas* – semi-fictional, data-driven representations of target users – are constructed and categorised. Equally important is transparency around how specific recommendations or automated decisions are made and under what conditions alternative outcomes might emerge.

AI can enhance the transparency of recommendation and opportunity algorithms by providing users with insights into why and how certain content is recommended or prioritised and by enabling them to adjust algorithmic parameters. This could involve explaining the factors used to determine content priorities, enabling users to be better informed and exercise greater control over their content consumption.

Providing users with this level of insight and agency enables them to recognise and counteract the embedded biases and preferences of algorithmic systems. It empowers them to shape their digital experience, mitigate the formation of algorithmic epistemic enclaves and engage with a broader spectrum of perspectives. Furthermore, such systems could alert users to subtle changes in their habitual behaviour which – rather than being exploited for advertisers' profits – could be used to enhance users' self-awareness and help prevent unwanted personal states or actions.

However, increased user control over algorithms introduces a degree of ambivalence. While offering new avenues for individual agency, it may simultaneously reinforce entrenched habitual patterns and preferences – manifesting in the persistence of a data-driven self, subjected to habitual, contractual behaviour and continuous monitoring, tracking and measurement. As Dewey cautioned, habits inherently contain a conservative dimension, with 'habits of opinion' proving particularly resistant to change. Ironically, efforts to enhance user self-control through algorithmic literacy may entrench, rather than disrupt, these deeply ingrained habits of mind.

For this reason, public-worthiness algorithms and corresponding regu-latory interventions are essential. They help ensure that transparency and user empowerment do not inadvertently reinforce the very dynamics they seek to challenge. Instead, they can support a digital environment oriented towards democratic values – encouraging deliberation, inclusivity and criti-cal engagement.

Development of Opportunity Algorithms. In contrast to conven-tional recommendation systems, which sustain engagement by anticipating and reinforcing user preferences, *opportunity algorithms* can serve as person-alised aides that help users navigate accessible content more effectively and meaningfully. Rather than reinforcing what users already like or know, these systems aim to expand informational horizons by exposing them to content they might not otherwise seek out but that carries social or civic value.

The fundamental question emerges: How can we determine what is truly public-worthy – worth knowing and discussing collectively – if we lack the opportunity to critically engage with it? While information is more abun-dant than ever, the time and cognitive capacity to process it meaningfully grow increasingly scarce. Opportunity algorithms can help bridge this gap by surfacing relevant, diverse and intentionally eye-opening content that fosters democratic discourse rather than algorithmic conformity.

Drawing on the concept of opportunity costs from microeconomic theory – used to measure potential loss when choosing one alternative over another – AI-driven opportunity algorithms could signal what users miss in terms of public-worthiness when no real choice is offered. By processing vast quanti-ties of content, these algorithms would assess the civic relevance of potentially visible content based on predefined criteria, such as societal impact, long-term consequences and political relevance. Through analysis of real-time and historical data, opportunity algorithms can forecast which topics are likely to gain importance in the near future, helping users to stay engaged with emerg-ing public debates. The goal is to provide users with authentic, pertinent information, helping them to identify, prioritise and engage with structur-ally significant issues. In doing so, these algorithms support more informed content selection while amplifying visibility for topics often marginalised in commercial information ecosystems.

By empowering users to choose public-worthy content and connecting them to context-rich discussions, opportunity algorithms can enhance both the quality of individual participation and the public-worthiness of digital discourse. Rooted in the concept of public-worthiness, these algorithms can foster a digital environment where users actively contribute to a more informed, inclusive and reflexive discourse.

Regulations to Strengthen Publicness. Legislative and non-legislative regulations play a crucial role in ensuring that digital platforms and services enabling gig publics uphold the principle of publicness, rather than devolving into systems defined by the self-sufficiency of private contractual relationships. Regulatory frameworks must be designed to transform platform governance – ensuring that platforms are accountable, function in the public interest and remain free from unchecked algorithmic bias and monopoly control concentrated in the hands of a few corporate actors.

To achieve this, clear obligations should be established for platform operators and content providers, including strict standards for algorithmic transparency and data privacy. Users must be empowered to understand how their data is collected, processed and used, as well as how recommendation algorithms determine visibility and relevance. These obligations are essential for rebuilding trust, enabling informed participation and safeguarding the democratic functions of digital platforms.

Countering the monopolisation of public discourse by platform giants requires a multipronged strategy: reorienting recommendation algorithms towards public-worthiness rather than profit, investing in independent, public-service media committed to in-depth reporting and pluralism of perspectives, and advancing regulatory initiatives such as the European Union's Digital Services Act (DSA), which mandates greater transparency in content moderation, advertising and algorithmic recommendation systems. However, the impact of such frameworks depends on effective enforcement, sustained oversight and the global coordination of comparable regulatory efforts to ensure that these principles translate into tangible protections for users and the publics, allowing users to understand and control how their data is used and how recommendation algorithms function. These regulatory obligations are essential to building trust, enabling informed participation and safeguarding the democratic function of digital platforms.

Reclaiming Online Autonomy through Collaborative Interventions. To counter corporate platform hegemony, users can adopt cooperative algorithmic strategies that defend online autonomy and foster digital self-determination. These include the creation of open-source recommendation systems that prioritise user needs and public-worthiness over engagement metrics, the development of browser extensions that audit and expose platform manipulation tactics and the organisation of 'data strikes' to disrupt exploitative data harvesting and profiling practices. Federated learning systems enable communities to train local algorithms on decentralised datasets, bypassing corporate data extraction. Users may also deploy adversarial algorithms designed to manipulate recommendation systems in order to surface marginalised or under-represented content, while cryptographic tools can support end-to-end algorithmic transparency. The goal of these cooperative, user-driven interventions is not to restrict data but to *reclaim* it – ensuring that its generation and distribution serve the interests of those who produce it and are affected by its use. Initiatives like Mozilla's 'Pledge for a Healthy Internet'[1] demonstrate that alternative trajectories are possible – prioritising inclusivity, civil discourse and epistemic virtues over engagement metrics and profit.

To effectively counter corporate platform hegemony through algorithmic resistance, users must cultivate both technical competencies and cooperative action frameworks. This requires robust algorithmic literacy programmes that demystify platform operations – teaching users how to audit recommendation systems, trace data extraction mechanisms and identify behavioural nudges embedded in interface design. However, these competencies become truly impactful only when paired with participatory design practices that empower communities to develop open-source alternatives – particularly collaborative filtering algorithms that prioritise public-worthiness metrics over engagement-driven performativity.

Some of the most promising interventions emerge at the intersection of technical innovation and organised resistance. Socio-technical 'adversarial hackathons' – bringing together technologists, activists and everyday users – can generate sophisticated counter-tools, including browser plugins that randomise clickstream data, simulate non-linear behaviour or inject noise into tracking systems. These efforts do not merely provide individual workarounds; they systematically degrade the predictive accuracy on which surveillance capitalism relies, thereby creating structural friction that disrupts platform dominance.

Cultivating Reflexive and Socially Engaged Citizens. For these strategies to succeed, thoughtful and informed user participation is indispensable. Just as literacy and newspaper reading catalysed the rise of the bourgeois public, today's citizens need new forms of civic literacy attuned to algorithmic logics, platform architectures and the socio-technical conditions that shape visibility, engagement and discourse.

Raising the general level and quality of education not only empowers citizens to lead autonomous, fulfilling lives – it is also a foundational precondition for democratic participation and scientific progress. As Gabriel Tarde noted, science both depends on and cultivates widespread education, linking epistemic advancement to public understanding. This view aligns with John

---

1 https://www.mozilla.org/en-US/about/manifesto/?utm_content=manifesto-referral &utm_medium=social&utm_source=twitter.

Dewey's democratic philosophy, which frames learning as intrinsic to all distinctly human activities and positions science as inherently democratic – a collective enterprise that enables informed deliberation and social cooperation (Dewey 1927/1946, 160).

While thinkers from John Stuart Mill and Alexis de Tocqueville to Walter Lippmann raised legitimate concerns about the public's limited capacity for rational autonomy – invoking concerns about the 'tyranny of the majority' or the 'phantom public' – Dewey retained a tempered optimism. His confidence rested in transformative education that fosters 'fundamental dispositions, intellectual and emotional, toward nature and fellow human beings' (Dewey 1915/2004, 354). In our era, this vision remains profoundly relevant: the survival of democratic societies hinges on cultivating epistemic virtues – critical thinking, dialogic reasoning and sound public judgement – that can transform gig publics into reflexive, self-governing collectives capable of sustaining democratic life. Where these educational foundations weaken, we witness the corrosive consequences: resurgent anti-intellectualism, populist demagoguery and conspiracy thinking – conditions that threaten the very fabric of democratic deliberation.

The Institutionalisation of Deliberation into Political Process through methods such as deliberative polling, it offers a powerful mechanism to counter the erosion of democratic discourse caused by algorithmic opacity. Unlike conventional polls, referendums, elections or online opinion data harvesting– which test, predict or even manipulate perceptions of public opinion in ways that mirror the opaque operations of recommendation algorithms – deliberative polling seeks to foster more authentic democratic engagement. It bridges the gap between public sentiment and policymaking by creating structured environments in which representative groups of citizens engage with balanced information and diverse perspectives before forming judgements (Fishkin 2018). Combined with other forms of considerate public reasoning, this process interrupts the performative dynamics that dominate digital platforms by depersonalising debate, reducing reliance on emotional soundbites and fostering authentic public judgement grounded in evidence and reason. While conventional polls are often assumed to produce 'independent opinions' – despite the subtle influence of the interview process – deliberative polls generate considered judgements that emerge through deliberation, informed reflection and dialogue.

Beyond improving policy outcomes, deliberative polling serves a crucial pedagogical function by modelling democratic dialogue and cultivating civic virtues. Participants develop critical thinking skills and learn to weigh trade-offs while engaging constructively with expert briefings and opposing viewpoints. This includes the development of critical literacy for navigating complex socio-technical environments, learning to interrogate algorithmic biases, resisting polarising narratives and engaging in reasoned collective judgement rather than reactionary discourse.

Over time, repeated exposure to such deliberative practices can raise the overall quality of public discourse. Moreover, when institutionalised – through citizens' assemblies, policy consultations or referendum processes – or even legally enacted (as with the Deliberative Polling Law adopted in Mongolia in 2017; Martinovich 2017), these practices can help stabilise the epistemic foundations of public life and restore legitimacy to democratic decision-making. However, their long-term success depends on parallel investments in civic education and digital literacy, aimed at cultivating a culture capable of sustaining reflexive and inclusive forms of publicness. Framed in this way, deliberative polling offers more than a technocratic innovation – it provides a pathway to reclaim public discourse from performative degradation and re-centre it on the collective task of democratic problem-solving.

These strategies for empowering citizens and enhancing the quality of public discourse point to a broader question – one that has guided this book throughout: What becomes of publicness in a world where platforms, habits and contracts govern the rhythms and expressions of civic life? We have seen how digital infrastructures convert public engagement into fragmented performances – short-lived, affectively charged and shaped by the logic of platform visibility. Yet this is not a narrative of inevitable decline. Rather, it is an invitation to reimagine public life under the complex conditions of algorithmic mediation.

The task before us is not merely to diagnose the forces that have hollowed out public discourse, but also to envision alternative practices that can sustain meaningful participation, critical reflection and collective agency. Publicness must be understood not simply as a normative ideal to be defended but as an ongoing social process – constructed, contested and maintained through specific cultural, institutional and technological arrangements. How we design and govern our digital environments will determine whether publics emerge as thoughtful, inclusive collectives or disintegrate into reactive crowds.

In the AI world, invigorating publicness requires confronting both technological complexity and institutional inertia. It calls for resisting the immediacy and spectacle that dominate online interaction and for affirming practices that foster commitment, listening and mutual recognition. These practices require time, effort and care – qualities often undervalued in surveillance capitalism but essential for any democratic future. They also demand democratic oversight, inclusive design and shared responsibility for how technologies shape public discourse.

To reclaim publicness in the algorithmic age is to confront fundamental questions about access, participation and power: Who has the capacity to determine what becomes visible in our digital agora? Whose voices are elevated or silenced? What forms of interactions are encouraged, and what kinds of knowledge are legitimised? These are not only technical or procedural issues to be solved through better platform design; they are deeply political questions, entangled with histories of exclusion and human struggles over visibility, agency and legitimisation. When platforms optimise for virality over veracity, or when states deploy AI for surveillance rather than solidarity, these are not neutral choices – they are political acts that demand democratic scrutiny.

The future of public life in the AI era hinges on our collective ability to cultivate spaces, practices and norms that support sustained, reflexive and inclusive engagement. This challenge is as much about reclaiming old wisdom as developing new solutions. It requires remembering that publicness has always been contested terrain, that technologies amplify but do not determine social outcomes and that the most important algorithms are still the human ones: our capacity for reason, for solidarity and for imagining collective futures.

This book has traced how gig publics form, are managed, and fragment in an age of algorithmic visibility and social acceleration – but also how they might be renewed. By resisting the flattening forces of digital automation that isolate and polarise, and by building conditions that nurture thoughtful dialogue and civic solidarity, we can create space for publics that do not merely flicker into view, but endure, resonate and co-create democratic opportunities and prospects. In this sense, invigorating publicness in the AI world is not about mastering ever-new tools but about reaffirming democracy's oldest and most vital promise: that people, when given the right conditions, can govern themselves wisely. The story of gig publics reminds us that the pursuit of inventing new forms of publicness and publics only truly makes sense when firmly rooted in the freedom of the public use of reason.

* * *

REFERENCES

Arendt, Hannah. 1958. *The Human Condition*. Chicago: The University of Chicago Press.

Arendt, Hannah. 1961. *Between Past and Future*. New York: Viking Press.

Asen, Robert. 2000. "Seeking the 'Counter' in Counterpublics." *Communication Theory* 10 (4): 424–446.

Aubin, France. 2014. "Between Public Space(s) and Public Sphere(s): An Assessment of Francophone Contributions." *Canadian Journal of Communication* 39 (1): 89–110.

Bentham, Jeremy. 1781/2000. *An Introduction to the Principles of Morals and Legislation*. Kitchener: Batoche Books.

Bentham, Jeremy. 1791/1843. "Of Publicity." Ch. II of A*n Essay on Political Tactics*. *The Works of Jeremy Bentham*, vol. 2, 577–589. Edinburgh: William Tait.

Bentham, Jeremy. 1812/1827. *Rationale of Judicial Evidence, Specially Applied to English Practice*. Edited by J. S. Mill. London: Hunt and Clarke.

Bentham, Jeremy. 1843. *Introductory View of the Rationale of Evidence, and Rationale of Judicial Evidence*. *The Works of Jeremy Bentham*, vol. 6. Edinburgh: William Tait.

Berelson, Bernard. 1949. "What Missing the Newspaper Means." In *Communications Research*, edited by P. Lazarsfeld and F. Stanton, 111–139. Charlotte: Harper.

Bobbio, Norberto. 1980/1989. *Democracy and Dictatorship*. Cambridge: Polity.

Boyle, Nicholas. 2012. "Private, Public, and Structural Change: The German Problem." In *Changing Perceptions of the Public Sphere*, edited by Christian J. Emden and David Midgley, 75–89. New York: Berghahn Books.

Browne, Harry. 2018. *Public Sphere*. Cork: Cork University Press.

Burtell, Matthew, and Thomas Woodside. 2023. "Artificial Influence: An Analysis of AI-Driven Persuasion." *arXiv preprint*. https://arxiv.org/pdf/2303.0872lvl.pdf.

CAIS. 2023. "Statement on AI Risk." Center for AI Safety. https://www.safe.ai/statement-on-ai-risk.

Calhoun, Craig. 2001. "Civil Society/Public Sphere: History of the Concept." In *International Encyclopedia of Social and Behavioral Sciences*, edited by N. J. Smelser, J. Wright, and P. B. Baltes, 1897–1903. Amsterdam: Elsevier.

Campbell, Donald T. 1958. "Common Fate, Similarity and Other Indices of the Status of Aggregates of Persons as Social Entities." *Systems Research and Behavioral Science* 3 (1): 14–25.

Dahlberg, Lincoln. 2018. "Visibility and the Public Sphere: A Normative Conceptualisation." *Javnost—The Public* 25 (1–2): 35–42.

Dewey, John. 1915/2004. *Democracy and Education. An Introduction to the Philosophy of Education*. Delhi: Aakar Books.

Dewey, John. 1927/1946. *The Public and Its Problems*. Chicago: Gateway.

Dhawan, Nikita. 2012. "Transnational Justice, Counterpublic Spheres and Alter-Globalization." *Localities* 2: 79–116.

DiSalvo, David. 2017. "Cognitive Bias. Recognizing and Managing Our Unconscious Biases." *The Pharos*. https://www.med.upenn.edu/inclusion-and-diversity/assets/user-content/cognitive-bias.pdf.

Durkheim, Émile. 1893/1984. *The Division of Labour in Society*. Houndmills: Macmillan.

Eisenegger, Mark, and Mike S. Schäfer. 2023. "Editorial: Reconceptualizing Public Sphere(s) in the Digital Age? On the Role and Future of Public Sphere Theory." *Communication Theory* 33 (2–3): 61–69.

Ellul, Jacques. 1954/1964. *The Technological Society*. New York: Vintage Books.

Felski, Rita. 1989. *Beyond Feminist Aesthetics: Feminist Literature and Social Change*. Cambridge, MA: Harvard University Press.

Festinger, Leon. 1957. *A Theory of Cognitive Dissonance*. Stanford: Stanford University Press.

Fishkin, James. 2018. *Democracy When the People Are Thinking: Revitalizing Our Politics Through Public Deliberation*. Oxford: Oxford University Press.

Fraser, Nancy. 1990. "Rethinking the Public Sphere: A Contribution to the Critique of Actually Existing Democracy." *Social Text* 25/26: 56–80.

Fraser, Nancy. 2007. "Transnationalizing the Public Sphere: On the Legitimacy and Efficacy of Public Opinion in a Post-Westphalian World." *Theory, Culture & Society* 24 (4): 7–30.

Friedman, Batya, and David G. Hendry. 2019. *Value Sensitive Design: Shaping Technology with Moral Imagination*. Cambridge, MA: MIT Press.

Galbraith, John K. 2006. "Free Market Fraud." *The Progressive*, April 12, 2006. https://progressive.org/latest/john-kenneth-galbraith-free-market-fraud/.

Ginsberg, Benjamin. 1989. "How Polling Transforms Public Opinion." In *Manipulating Public Opinion*, edited by M. Margolis and G. A. Mauser, 271–293. Pacific Grove, CA: Brooks/Cole.

Glick, Ira, and Sidney J. Levy. 1962/2017. *Living with Television*. Milton Park: Routledge.

Gouldner, Alvin W. 1976. *The Dialectic of Ideology and Technology: The Origins, Grammar and Future*. New York: The Seabury Press.

Habermas, Jürgen. 1962/1990. *Strukturwandel der Öffentlichkeit*. Frankfurt: Suhrkamp.

Habermas, Jürgen. 1962/1991. *The Structural Transformation of the Public Sphere*. Cambridge: MIT Press.

Habermas, Jürgen. 1992/1996. *Between Facts and Norms*. Cambridge: MIT Press.

Habermas, Jürgen. 2022. "Reflections and Hypotheses on a Further Structural Transformation of the Political Public Sphere." *Theory, Culture & Society* 39 (4): 145–171.

Hansen, Miriam. 1993. "Foreword." In O. Negt and A. Kluge, *Public Sphere and Experience: Toward an Analysis of the Bourgeois and Proletarian Public Sphere*, ix–xlix. Minneapolis: University of Minnesota Press.

Harrisson, Tom. 1940. "What Is Public Opinion?" *Political Quarterly* 11 (4): 368–383.

Hegel, G. W. F. 1821/2001. *Philosophy of Right*. Translated by S. W. Dyde. Kitchener: Batoche Books.

Hume, David. 1741/1777. "Of the First Principles of Government." In *Essays, Moral, Political, and Literary*, edited by Eugene F. Miller, 32–37. Indiannapolis: Liberty Fund.

Hume, David. 1748/2007. *An Enquiry Concerning Human Understanding*. Oxford: Oxford University Press.

Jackson, Sarah J., and Daniel Kreiss. 2023. "Recentering Power: Conceptualizing Counterpublics and Defensive Publics." *Communication Theory* 33 (2–3): 102111.

James, William. 1890/2007. *The Principles of Psychology*, vol 1, 2. New York: Cosimo Classics.

Kaluža, Jernej. 2022. "Habitual Generation of Filter Bubbles: Why Is Algorithmic Personalisation Problematic for the Democratic Public Sphere?" *Javnost—The Public* 29 (3): 267–283.

Kant, Immanuel. 1784. "An Answer to the Question: What Is Enlightenment?" https://www.marxists.org/reference/subject/ethics/kant/enlightenment.htm.

Kant, Immanuel. 1795/1939. *Perpetual Peace*. New York: Columbia University Press.

Kant, Immanuel. 1798 /1979. *The Conflict of the Faculties*. New York: Abaris Books.

Lang, Kurt. 1962/2017. "Introduction to the Aldinetransaction Edition." In Ira Glick and Sidney J. Levy, *Living with Television*. Milton Park: Routledge.

Lasswell, Harold D. 1957. "The Impact of Public Opinion on Our Society." *Public Opinion Quarterly* 21 (1): 33–38.

Lipka, Michael, and Elisa Shearer. 2023. "Audiences Are Declining for Traditional News Media in the U.S. – With Some Exceptions." Washington, DC: Pew Research Center. https://www.pewresearch.org/short-reads/2023/11/28/audiences-are-declining-for -traditional-news-media-in-the-us-with-some-exceptions/.

Lippmann, Walter. 1922/1991. *Public Opinion*. New Brunswick: Transaction Publishers.

Machiavelli, Niccolò. 1513/2006. *The Prince*. https://www.gutenberg.org/files/1232 /1232-h/1232-h.htm.

Martinovich, Milenko. 2017. Collaboration at Stanford Leads to Mongolian Parliament Passing Law on Public Opinion Polling. https://medium.com/@StanfordCDDRL /collaboration-at-stanford-leads-to-mongolian-parliament-passing-law-on-public -opinion-polling-983d12966857.

Marx, Karl. 1842/1974. "Die Verhandlungen des 6. rheinischen Landtags: Debatten über Pressefreiheit und Publikation der Landständischen Verhandlungen." In *Marx-Engels Werke*, 1:28–77. Berlin: Dietz Verlag. On Freedom of the Press. https://www .marxists.org/archive/marx/works/1842/free-press/.

Marx, Karl. 1843/1974. "Rechtfertigung des + +– – Korrespondenten von der Mosel." In *Marx-Engels Werke*, 1:172–199. Berlin: Dietz Verlag.

Marx Ferree, Myra, William A. Gamson, Jürgen Gerhards, and Dieter Rucht. 2002. "Four Models of the Public Sphere in Modern Democracies." *Theory and Society* 31: 289–324.

McLuhan, Marshall. 1964/1994. *Understanding Media: The Extensions of Man*. Cambridge, MA: The MIT Press.

Mill, John Stuart. 1859/2001. *On Liberty*. Kitchener: Batoche Books.

Mill, John Stuart. 1861/1991. "Considerations on Representative Government." In *On Liberty and Other Essays*, edited by John Gray, 203–467. Oxford: Oxford University Press. https://www.gutenberg.org/cache/epub/5669/pg5669-images.html.

Mills, C. Wright. 1956/1999. *The Power Elite*. Oxford: Oxford University Press.

Mumford, Lewis. 1934. *Technics and Civilization*. London: George Routledge & Sons.

Murdock, Graham, and Peter Golding. 1989. "Information Poverty and Political Inequality: Citizenship in the Age of Privatized Communication." *Journal of Communication* 39 (3): 180–195.

Negt, Oskar, and Alexander Kluge. 1972. *Öffentlichkeit und Erfahrung. Zur Organisationsanalyse von bürgerlicher und proletarischer Öffentlichkeit*. Frankfurt: Suhrkamp Verlag.

Newman, Nic, Kirsten Eddy, Craig T. Robertson, and Rasmus Kleis Nielsen. 2023. *Reuters Institute Digital News Report 2023*. Reuters Institute for the Study of Journalism.

https://reutersinstitute.politics.ox.ac.uk/sites/default/files/2023-06/Digital_News _Report_2023.pdf.

Nimmo, Ben. 2024. *AI and Covert Influence Operations: Latest Trends.* OpenAI. https:// downloads.ctfassets.net/kftzwdyauwt9/5IMxzTmUclSOAcWUXbkVrK/3cfab51 8e6b10789ab8843bcca18b633/Threat_Intel_Report.pdf.

O'Mahony, Patrick. 2021. "Habermas and the Public Sphere: Rethinking a Key Theoretical Concept." *European Journal of Social Theory* 24 (4): 485–506.

Papacharissi, Zizi. 2015. *Affective Publics: Sentiment, Technology, and Politics.* New York: Oxford University Press.

Park, Robert E. 1904/1972. *The Crowd and the Public.* Edited by H. Elsner, Jr. Chicago: University of Chicago Press.

Parsons, Talcott. 1942. "Propaganda and Social Control." *Psychiatry* 5 (4): 551–572.

Parsons, Talcott. 1963. "On the Concept of Influence." *Public Opinion Quarterly* 27 (1): 37–62.

Pew Research Center. 2023. Podcasts as a Source of News and Information. April 18. https://www.pewresearch.org/journalism/2023/04/18/podcasts-as-a-source-of -news-and-information/.

Pew Research Center. 2023a. Newspapers Fact Sheet. November 10. https://www .pewresearch.org/journalism/fact-sheet/newspapers/.

Plato. 360 B.C.E. *Phaedrus.* Translated by Benjamin Jowett. https://classics.mit.edu/ Plato/phaedrus.html.

Reichel, Chloe. 2018. "Civic Engagement Declines when Local Newspapers Shut Down." *The Journalist's Resource.* https://journalistsresource.org/politics-and-government/ local-newspapers-civic-engagement/.

Ryan, Johnny, and Wolfie Christl. 2023. *Europe's Hidden Security Crisis.* Irish Council for Civil Liberties. https://www.iccl.ie/wp-content/uploads/2023/11/Europes-hidden -security-crisis.pdf.

Searls, Doc. 2012. *The Intention Economy: When Customers Take Charge.* Brighton, MA: Harvard Business Review Press.

Simon, Herbert A. 1971. "Designing Organizations for an Information-Rich World." In *Computers, Communications, and the Public Interest,* edited by M. Greenberger, 38–72. Baltimore: Johns Hopkins Press.

Sorokin, Pitirim A. 1941/1992. *The Crisis of Our Age.* Oxford: Oneworld Publications.

Sorokin, Pitirim A. 1957/1970. *Social and Cultural Dynamics.* Boston: Porter Sargent Publisher.

Splichal, Slavko. 1981. *Množično komuniciranje med svobodo in odtujitvijo* (Mass Communication between Freedom and Alienation). Maribor: Obzorja.

Splichal, Slavko. 2012. *Transnationalization of the Public Sphere and the Fate of the Public.* New York: Hampton.

Splichal, Slavko. 2018. "Publicness–Privateness: The Liquefaction of 'The Great Dichotomy'." *Javnost—The Public* 25 (1–2): 1–10.

Splichal, Slavko. 2022. *Datafication of Public Opinion and the Public Sphere.* London: Anthem.

Statista. 2025. Most Popular Social Networks Worldwide as of February 2025, by Number of Monthly Active Users. https://www.statista.com/statistics/272014/global -social-networks-ranked-by-number-of-users//.

Stearns, Josh. 2022. Strong Local Journalism = More People Turning out to Vote. Democracy Fund. https://democracyfund.org/idea/how-we-know-journalism-is -good-for-democracy/.

Stitini, Oumaima, Iván García-Magariño, Soulaimane Kaloun, and Omar Benchar. 2023. "Towards Ideal and Efficient Recommendation Systems Based on the Five Evaluation Concepts Promoting Serendipity." *Journal of Advances in Information Technology* 14 (4): 701–717.

Sue, Roger. 2016. *La contre-société*. Paris: Les liens qui libèrent.

Tarde, Gabriel. 1901/1989. *L'Opinion et la foule*. Paris: Les Presses universitaires de France.

Tönnies, Ferdinand. 1887/2020. *Community and Society*. Edited by C. P. Loomis. Augusta, GA: Mockingbird Press.

Tönnies, Ferdinand. 1909/1961. *Custom. An Essay on Social Codes*. Chicago: Henry Regnery.

Tönnies, Ferdinand. 1916. "Zur Theorie der öffentlichen Meinung." *Schmollers Jahrbuch für Gesetzgebung, Verwaltung und Volkswirtschaft im Deutschen Reiche* 40 (4): 2001–2030.

Tönnies, Ferdinand. 1922. *Kritik der öffentlichen Meinung*. Berlin: Julius Springer.

Trenz, Hans-Jörg. 2024. *Democracy and the Public Sphere: From Dystopia Back to Utopia*. Bristol: Bristol University Press.

van Dijck, José. 2009. "Users Like You? Theorizing Agency in User-Generated Content." *Media, Culture & Society* 31 (1): 41–58.

Warner, Michael. 2002. "Publics and Counterpublics." *Public Culture* 14 (1): 49–90.

Washington Post. 2021. "Local News Deserts Are Expanding: Here's What We'll Lose." https://www.washingtonpost.com/magazine/interactive/2021/local-news-deserts-expanding/.

Weber, Max. 1921/2019. *Economy and Society*. Cambridge, MA: Harvard University Press.

Zuboff, Shoshana. 2019. *The Age of Surveillance Capitalism: The Fight for a Human Future at the New Frontier of Power*. New York: PublicAffairs/Perseus Books.

INDEX

www.ingramcontent.com/pod-product-compliance
Lightning Source LLC
Chambersburg PA
CBHW030652270326
41929CB00007B/324